SPIRIT
SOUL & BODY

SPIRIT

SOUL & BODY

LESTER SUMRALL

WHITAKER
HOUSE

Unless otherwise indicated, all Scripture quotations are taken from the King James Version (KJV) of the Bible.

Scripture quotations marked (NIV) are from the Holy Bible, *New International Version,* © 1973, 1978, 1984 by the International Bible Society. Used by permission.

Scripture quotations marked (AMP) are from the Amplified New Testament, © 1954, 1958, 1987, by the Lockman Foundation, and are used by permission; or are from the Amplified Bible, Old Testament, © 1962, 1964 by Zondervan Publishing House, and used by permission.

SPIRIT, SOUL, AND BODY

ISBN: 0-88368-375-X
Printed in the United States of America
© 1995 by Lester Sumrall

Whitaker House
30 Hunt Valley Circle
New Kensington, PA 15068

Library of Congress Cataloging-in-Publication Data

Sumrall, Lester Frank, 1913–
  Spirit, soul, and body / Lester Sumrall.
      p. cm.
Originally published: ©1995.
  ISBN 0-88368-375-X (pbk.)
 1. Man (Christian theology) 2. Christian life. I. Title.
  BT701.3 .S86 2002
  233'.5—dc21
                                            2002000276

1 2 3 4 5 6 7 8 9 10 11 12 / 09 08 07 06 05 04 03 02

Contents

1
The New Thing

◆●◆

The great psalmist said in Psalm 8:4, *"What is man, that thou art mindful of him? and the son of man, that thou visitest him?"*

Evidently the psalmist suddenly became alarmed by the immensity of this thing called man. For six thousand years this question has been on the lips of humans, "What is man that You give such attention to him, God?" The whole Bible was written primarily for man. It is not a book on astrology or astronomy. It is not a book on sciences; it is a book about man.

Possibly there is no truth whose time has so fully come as the truth about the total man. Maybe there has never been such eagerness in our land to understand this truth as there is at this moment. I am delighted at this. This truth can resolve personal problems. It can resolve family, church, and community problems. When we know the truth of the total man, we get to the very core and center of all human problems. It is not enough to have a definition; we must have an application of how this truth works. Then it is really useful to us.

There are three major areas of education with which all of us must grapple.

Who Is God?

The first and primary area is God. A person who does not know God has not actually started to live. How can a person say he knows how to live if he does not know God? I believe firmly that God made this earth, and we ought to know something about Him. When you see a watch, would you like to know the maker? Have you ever wondered how God makes humans? The greatest knowledge that a human can have in this world is a knowledge of God. Very few people ever get to know God. Many people know about God, but they do not know God. If you are not willing to concentrate, penetrate, and seek with your total being to know God, you will not know Him.

The greatest revelation of God is in the Bible. You should begin at the first page and read to the last page. What a study you would enjoy!

Atheists, communists, and agnostics do not know God! Sinners do not know Him either! Yet we do not really live until we begin to know God. To know Him is to understand what life is all about. God was so desirous that we get to know Him that He sent His Son to represent Him, so that in the Son we would see God. John 3:16 says, *"For God so loved the world, that he gave his only begotten Son, that whosoever believeth in him should not perish, but have everlasting life."*

Know Your Fellowman

The second vast area of information for every human is knowing our fellowman. It is amazing that we can live with humans all our lives and not know anything about them. Have you ever heard a man say after living with a woman for fifty years, "I don't understand her"? He thought he did when he married her, but somewhere along the line, communication broke down.

We would not have wars if we knew one another. The Russians are nice people; I have lived with them. The Germans are lovely people; I have lived with them, too. All nations are full of nice people. If we had a knowledge of one another, there would not be wars or any other kind of friction. If there was a complete understanding between management and labor, there would not be all the friction we have. It is an understanding of our fellowman that we need, but so many times we do not see what makes this person hurt, that person sad, or another person feel like we do not care for him. We do not seek to understand what makes others happy or unhappy. Until we know who God is and learn to understand our fellowman, we have not started to live.

Know Yourself

The third great key to understanding successful living is to know yourself. Very few humans know themselves at all. I struggled honestly, sincerely, and continually for more than twenty years to understand the difference between spirit and soul. I asked almost every prominent religious leader whom I met in my travels throughout the whole world. As soon as I would meet a biblical scholar I would say, "What is the spirit of a human? Where does it reside? How does it manifest itself? When does a person receive his spirit—at birth or rebirth?"

Do you know I could not find a single person who could tell me? Finally, the answer came by revelation.

Your Spirit—The Born-Again Nature

One morning, about two o'clock, I was begging God to tell me. God spoke very beautifully to me and said, "Your spirit is your born-again nature."

I replied, "That sounds very simple." Then, suddenly the whole great truth bubbled and burst open right in my face. I began to explain it to others in camp meetings and conventions all over the country. I began to talk about the total man. Who he is and what he has become are very common subjects today, but I had never heard one sermon on it for the first thirty years of my ministry.

David asked in Psalm 8:4–6,

What is man, that thou art mindful of him? and the son of man, that thou visitest him? For thou hast made him a little lower than the angels, and hast crowned him with glory and honour. Thou madest him to have dominion over the works of thy hands; thou hast put all things under his feet.

Man's Composite Nature

I had read that Scripture dozens of times and did not understand it until God told me what the composite nature of a human person really is. Its meaning did not come to me until God showed me that the spirit and soul are distinctly different. Suddenly I understood what God meant when He said, *"I crowned man with glory and honor"* (Psalm 8:5). Man has dominion over the works of God's hands. This means that we, as humans, have dominion. God has put all things under our feet. Would it not be wonderful if we lived up to all the things that belong to us?

Hebrews 4:12 says, *"For the word of God is quick* [the old English word *"quick"* does not mean "fast"; it means "moving" or "living"], *and powerful, and sharper than any twoedged sword, piercing even to the dividing asunder of soul and spirit."*

If we are ever going to know the difference between our soul and spirit, it will come from the Word of God. We can study psychology in all the universities of the world and not come up with an answer, because God says His Word has the answer.

If we do not get our answer from the Bible, we will be without an answer for the rest of our lives.

First Thessalonians 5:23 says, *"And the very God of peace sanctify you wholly; and I pray God your whole spirit and soul and body be preserved blameless unto the coming of our Lord Jesus Christ."*

Outside of the Bible, man is a dualism or two-part creature.

Psychiatry, psychology, and philosophy teach that man is two parts. They think he is inside and outside, topside and bottomside. The Word of God says that man is three.

I really feel that God is doing a new thing on the earth today in a remarkable and wonderful way. God is exploding revelation in this end time. This truth has not been fully taught in our generation.

Historical Truth and Pertinent Truth

There are two embodiments of truth. One of these truths is historical truth, and the other is pertinent truth. We should have a thorough comprehension of this.

Historical truth is unrelated to your destiny. For example, once there was a man named Noah who built a big boat. Noah was not a shipbuilder, but God gave him the blueprints and taught him how to build it. Until 1850 A.D. nobody ever built a boat as big as his. We accept this story as history, but it has nothing to do with the peace that is in our hearts now. It has nothing to do with the joy that is in our soul. It is true, but it is historical truth.

Pertinent truth is the opposite of that. It has to do with the fact that God loves you, He gave His Son for you, and you can be saved forever right now!

There are literally worlds of *pertinent truth* in the Bible. They have to do with your joy, happiness, and peace. The doctrine of the total man belongs in the column of pertinent truth. You must understand yourself to be a successful Christian. You have to know who you are before you can direct yourself. It is possible that 95 percent of all the Christians in our land (even though they are born again and their spirits are alive) still live, act, and think in their Adamic nature. They are living in the old man. Within them abides the secret of the new man, but they have not been taught pertinent truth; they are living in the ways and the feelings of the old Adamic nature. God is now calling them to a new life in Christ Jesus. This is why I want to lead you into the exploration of the third great area of truth: the understanding of ourselves—the total man.

2
The New Man

◆●◆

In my ministry, I seek to give almost all of my total time to *pertinent truth.* I feel that my life has been called by God. I am called to dig deep within my personal being for vital truth that will help you to be a better person today. My calling is to show you how to live a victorious life.

While I was waiting for a plane in a New York City airport, I was looking through the book department. There I saw a book on *How to Be a Carpenter.* I cannot saw a straight line or screw a screw, so I did not buy that book. Next I found *How to Be a Cook.* I cannot cook either, so I did not buy that one. As I looked I thought, "Isn't it amazing? Here are books on how to do all these things, except one thing is missing—how to live!" I said, "Wait a minute! They have missed the big one, HOW DO YOU LIVE?" God said, "That is your job!" In this study, I am going to help you understand yourself and therefore know how to live. I want to make you aware of the three-dimensional nature of the human personality. As long as you treat the human personality as a dualism, you will never discover it. A psychologist or psychiatrist might be able to pick you to pieces, but he will not know how to put you back together again. He thinks that the whole of the inner being is soul. He does not even know that man has a spirit. This is a very sad situation because man's biggest problems are spiritual. Doctors have not yet discovered that dimension.

In the Likeness of God

God's first words about the total man are in the first chapter of the Bible. *"And God said, Let us make man in our image, after our likeness"* (Genesis 1:26). When you see God, He will be about your size. He will have two eyes, one nose, two ears, and four fingers and a thumb on each hand. In His earthly life, Jesus was totally average and normal. When we get to heaven, the Bible says we will be like Jesus. It also says that we are made in His image and likeness. God was afraid you would not catch it the first time, so He said it twice.

Man Is Created to Rule

Then God said in Genesis 1:26, *"And let them have dominion."* Now maybe the greatest truth that I am going to teach you about this total man is your powerful relationship to this earth. We actually own this earth, yet we bargain it away to the devil. This earth is ours, and in the millennial kingdom we are to rule on this earth just like Adam ruled it. He lost it, but Jesus is going to give it back to us. Man is a dominion person. Every man is a king, and every woman is a queen on the face of this earth. God made man to have dominion, and He made him like Himself—in three parts. God is the sovereign of this total universe, and His eternal wisdom conceived the desire to create an intellectual, soulical creature of moral responsibility and integrity.

God Has a Personal Spirit

God has been called a spirit, and He is a spirit. God's Spirit was active in the Creation. The Bible says that the Spirit of God moved upon the waters. We find His Spirit in redemption. John 3:16 says, *"For God so loved the world, that he gave his only begotten Son, that whosoever believeth in him should not perish, but have everlasting life."* We find His Spirit functioning in that relationship. He communicated with Noah, saying that there would be a flood. He communicated with Abraham. He communicated with Paul and John. It was through His Spirit that He communicated Himself to them.

God the Father Has a Soul

This is the divine soul of perfection, never tainted with sin, nor clouded by doubt. His mind is greater than all human comprehension ever has been or ever will be. His emotions are evident in the Scriptures. He has shown joy and anger. He has every emotion that you find in a human person. God's emotions are never out of place or wrongly used. Rather, they are divinely used from His own life. God, in His soulical parts, identifies Himself with man in that He has a mind, emotions, and a will.

God Has a Body

God's body is very likely about the same size as Jesus' body. When Stephen saw Jesus standing beside the Father, he described the scene as though they were natural together. He did not say that the Father was a giant compared to His Son. Acts 7:56–57 says,

> Behold, I see the heavens opened, and the Son of man
> standing on the right hand of God. Then they cried
> out with a loud voice, and stopped their ears, and ran
> upon him with one accord.

God has hands. With His hands He made Adam. *He
has eyes.*

> For the eyes of the LORD run to and fro throughout
> the whole earth, to show himself strong in the behalf
> of them whose heart is perfect toward him.
>   (2 Chronicles 16:9)

God has a face. "And Jacob called the name of the place
Peniel: for I have seen God face to face, and my life is preserved" (Genesis 32:30).
He was seen by Moses and the elders in Exodus
24:9–11,

> Then went up Moses, and Aaron, Nadab, and Abihu,
> and seventy of the elders of Israel: and they saw the
> God of Israel: and there was under his feet as it were
> a paved work of a sapphire stone, and as it were the
> body of heaven in his clearness. And upon the nobles
> of the children of Israel he laid not his hand: also they
> saw God, and did eat and drink.

That is one of the most remarkable Scriptures in the
whole Bible. Exodus 33:11 says, "And the LORD spake unto
Moses face to face, as a man speaketh unto his friend."
God has fingers.

> In the same hour came forth fingers of a man's hand,
> and wrote over against the candlestick upon the plas-
> ter of the wall of the king's palace: and the king saw
> the part of the hand that wrote.   (Daniel 5:5)

The king saw the hand of God as it wrote.

And he gave unto Moses, when he had made an end of communing with him upon mount Sinai, two tables of testimony, tables of stone, written with the finger of God.   (Exodus 31:18)

God has feet. He walked with Adam.

And they heard the voice of the LORD God walking in the garden in the cool of the day: and Adam and his wife hid themselves from the presence of the LORD God amongst the trees of the garden.   (Genesis 3:8)

We find in Genesis 5:22–24 that God walked with Enoch.

And Enoch walked with God after he begat Methuselah three hundred years, and begat sons and daughters: and all the days of Enoch were three hundred sixty and five years: and Enoch walked with God: and he was not; for God took him.

When you and I get to heaven, we are going to find that God has a body like we have and a soul like we have and a spirit like we have. God made us in His own likeness and His own image. That is precisely the truth. We will understand it all much better when we see Him face-to-face. Until that time, we accept the Word of God as it is.

Many people think that God is a floating cloud or a ghost or something like steam coming out of a kettle, but God is like us. When we see God, we are going to see that He has the same wholeness and total man we have.

God has a voice. "And lo a voice from heaven, saying, This is my beloved Son, in whom I am well pleased" (Matthew 3:17). So we find that God's voice was heard by many people. They all were standing there and heard the voice of God speaking and pointing toward Jesus, *"This is my beloved Son, in whom I am well pleased."* We read in Exodus 33:23, *"And I will take away mine hand, and thou shalt see my back parts: but my face shall not be seen."* Here we find that God showed Moses His back parts. That means He has a back and shoulders. He has all the different parts of a personal being.

In Genesis 18:3-8, Abraham was talking to God, who had not yet revealed His identity.

> *And [Abraham] said, My Lord, if now I have found favour in thy sight, pass not away, I pray thee, from thy servant: Let a little water, I pray you, be fetched, and wash your feet, and rest yourselves under the tree: and I will fetch a morsel of bread, and comfort ye your hearts; after that ye shall pass on: for therefore are ye come to your servant. And they said, So do, as thou hast said. And Abraham hastened into the tent unto Sarah, and said, Make ready quickly three measures of fine meal, knead it, and make cakes upon the hearth. And Abraham ran unto the herd, and fetched a calf tender and good, and gave it unto a young man; and he hasted to dress it. And he took butter, and milk, and the calf which he had dressed, and set it before them; and he stood by them under the tree, and they did eat.*

Here we see that God had all the bodily parts of a man. He had feet that needed to be washed. He had legs that needed to be rested. He had a mouth and digestive tract to eat the meal.

God Identifies with Man

This is the most glorious thing that we could ever realize, that the One who put the universe and worlds into existence is totally identifiable with you and me. That makes me realize that you and I have never known the power that we could get from God—the power of speech. God spoke worlds into existence. He spoke constellations into existence. He spoke the starry domes of the heavens into existence. He did all this by the words of His mouth. The amazing thing is that we have mouths and words, and, if we had not fallen into sin through Adam, we would have had creativity equal with God's. The Lord Jesus is going to redeem us back into a divine relationship with God. We do not know how glorious it is going to be, but we can be sure that the creativity and similarity will be there. We will see God and understand that He has a spirit, that we have His Spirit within us, and that we have equal spirits with God.

We will also realize that God has soulical parts, and we will demonstrate our soulical parts along with God. Our whole beings will conform to the Almighty. Then we will live and dwell with Him. We will rejoice with Him throughout all eternity.

God the Father has all the qualities of a human being. The Bible substantiates them, especially the bodily parts. When we cannot see those bodily parts with our natural eyes, it makes some of us believe that He does not have bodily parts. His bodily parts are not related to corporeality. They are not related to the dust and minerals under our feet. They are related to what Jesus was when He was transfigured on the Mount and the glory gleamed through the tissues of His skin, and what He was on the day of Resurrection. Those are the qualities that God the Father has.

In our resurrected bodies, our total bodily parts will be exactly like the Lord Jesus and like God the Father.

Creation, Not Evolution

Science spends millions of hours working on rats and monkeys trying to understand us. That shows you how confused so-called intelligent men can be. When God says, *"Let us make man in our image, after our likeness: and let them have dominion"* (Genesis 1:26), that means man did not evolve. Man did not come up from something else. Man is the same today as he was from the beginning. The devil will put it into anybody's heart to think anything as beautiful as a human person came from anything as ignominious as a small four-footed beast or creature of the earth.

You could believe it the other way, that man dropped off a pedestal and found his way down to where he is today. That might seem to be something to look into, but there is no evidence on the face of this earth that there is anything evolving—none at all! Even the sun gets darker every day. The sun is actually burning itself out. None of the stars are getting brighter; they are burning themselves out. This shows you that the total universe is a creative act of God. It did not come up; it came down from God out of heaven.

Man Was to Rule by Spirit

The magnificent truth is that God created man in his triune being to rule over the earth and everything on this planet. This rulership was to be a function of his spirit. It is not the function of his soulical parts; man was intended to commune with his Maker by his spirit, and to rule this earth through his spirit. This is vitally important because if we do not get this point, we will never understand what the unregenerate man is today. We will have no comprehension of why he is what he is if we do not realize that God created man to live by his spirit and not by his soulical parts.

Satan Attacks

We do not know how long Adam and Eve may have lived in the Garden before the devil came to them and said, "You don't have to obey God." When he came to Eve in the Garden, he had to deal with the total trinity of her personality. First he attacked her body, the weakest part of the human personality. "Hey, woman, look at that fruit. Isn't it pretty? It is good eating, too. Taste it!" Next, he said, "You know it will make you smart?" This was an attack on Eve's soul. "You want to know something else? You will be like God." This was his blow against her spirit. So he hit her body; down she went. Then he struck her soul; down she went. Finally he landed a crippling blow against her spirit. He hit her three ways in the temptation, and she fell all three times. Defeated—body, soul, and spirit.

Four thousand years later the same tempter, the devil, met Jesus. After Jesus had nothing to eat for forty days, he said, "Man, You're hungry, aren't You? I know how much power You have; take that stone and make Yourself a nice piece of French bread. It would taste good with that good crust on it." Rather than smacking His lips like Eve would have done, Jesus retorted in Matthew 4:4, *"Man shall not live by bread alone, but by every word that proceedeth out of the mouth of God."*

Satan did not quit there. He took Him to the pinnacle of the temple and said, "You know, for the head of an evangelistic society, You're kind of a poor one. I haven't seen Your name in the *Jerusalem Times* at all. You do not have a following. Now if You will jump off here in front of all these people, they will put that on the front page of the paper. You know the angels will hold You up." Jesus responded in Matthew 4.7, *"Thou shalt not tempt the Lord thy God."* Then the devil gave Jesus the third test. He said, "I'll give You all the nations of the world." Satan was thinking, "I could not get Your body. I could not get Your soul, but if I could get to Your spirit...." Jesus said in Matthew 4:10, *"Get thee hence, Satan: for it is written, Thou shalt worship the Lord thy God, and him only shalt thou serve."*

It is important to realize that man lives in these three areas of personality, because Satan still attacks like he did with Eve and Jesus. If we do not defend all three areas of personality, we will not live in the dominion God intended for us. Rather, we will become prisoners of war in Satan's camp.

3
The Divine Purpose

———————————◆●◆———————————

God said that on the day Adam ate of the forbidden fruit he would die. Adam ate of that tree, yet his body did not die. It lived another nine hundred and thirty years. He fathered sons, daughters, grandsons, and granddaughters. His soul did not die because his mind remained clear. He had named all the animals and remembered their names. He could give a name to every flower on the face of the earth and remember the name of that flower. His emotions did not die, because there was great rage in his family. Emotions must have been very strong—anger, hate, and murder. Man's willpower did not die. Men continued to do as they pleased. They chose not to serve God and brought the Flood. So we see that man did not die in his soulical parts. What was it that died? Immediately when he transgressed, Adam hid from God. Even to this day every sinner hides from God.

The Day the Spirit of Man Died

As soon as Eve sinned, she said, "Oh, I'm naked." She was ashamed and began to look for fig leaves to put together for cover. Adam and Eve had lost God's presence. They lost their relationship with

God. Their consciences became a second-rate function that they could mess around with and disobey. Before, the human conscience had flowed magnificently and beautifully with God. *It was the third person of the triune being inside man that died.*

When the spirit of man died, his relationship with God died. When God thrust him out of the Garden of Eden, man was operating in his soul and body. Adam's nature changed from a spiritual being into a soulical being. That is the reason Jesus is called "the last Adam." He brings you back to the very place where man lost his glory. He clothes you again with a glorious robe of righteousness, because you have returned to the place where the third part of your being comes alive in God. You are a new creature in Christ Jesus. When you come to that place, you learn how to function there. It does not come automatically. If you want to function in your soulical parts, you can do it.

Operating on Two Cylinders

After their transgression, our forebears, Adam and Eve, had two parts—the body and the soul. That is all you were born with. When you are born on this earth, you are born with two parts, not three. You have to be born again to have a spirit. When Jesus told Nicodemus that, he could not believe it. He was an old man, possibly ninety years old. He was a member of the Supreme Court in Israel, and a man who kept the commandments of God. Nicodemus loved the young preacher named Jesus. He came inquiring, "Rabbi, we know You came from heaven." Jesus did not even answer him. He simply said, "You must be born again." Nicodemus questioned, "Now young rabbi, my mother has been dead quite a few years, and I'm about ninety. What is it You just said about being born again?" Jesus said, "There is a birth of the natural flesh and a birth of the spirit. You must be born again." (See John 3:1–9.) Ephesians 2:1 says that He has revived you who were dead in sins and trespasses. In Adam, we have the death of the human spirit. Man has a soulish, Adamic mind, emotions, and will. His five senses in their natural state will not serve God, do not want to serve God, and have to be commanded by the spirit to serve God before they will. That is the situation every one of us are born into whether we like it or not.

Who's on the Throne of Your Soul?

Paul said in 1 Corinthians 15:45, *"And so it is written, The first man Adam was made a living soul; the last Adam was made a quickening spirit."* You are two persons within your physical body. You have within you the first man, Adam. His blood is in our veins. We also have within us, as Christians, the last Adam, which is a quickening spirit. Each of your two inner portions has a throne. Your soul has a throne. The throne of your soul is your mind. When a person comes to me and wants to be delivered from demon power, invariably I have to relieve that power from his mind. That is the soul's throne, and the devil always looks for a throne. From the very beginning up in heaven, it was a throne he wanted. Even when he has an Antichrist, he'll get a big throne on which to seat him. He is totally throne-conscious. When he is in hell forever, he will be sitting on a throne down there. Hundreds of people whom I have prayed for said it felt like they had bands around their heads. The devil wants to control the throne of the mind. So when I set a person free, I set his mind free first.

The Spirit Has a Throne

Man has another throne. It is the throne of his spirit. This is the throne I desired for so many years. Where is the throne of man's spirit? It is in his belly. Jesus said in John 7:38, *"Out of his belly shall flow rivers of living water."* He did not say it would come out of your head or your heart. He said that out of your belly rivers of living water will flow. God has chosen this little part of your being to establish a throne. All happiness flows out of there. You cannot really laugh unless it comes from the belly or spirit. You can say, "He-he-he!" but that is from Hollywood. It is tinsel and not real. When you are really happy you laugh, "Ha-ha-ha!" Did you know that when you receive a spiritual language from heaven it flows out of your spirit? No one has ever spoken to the heavenly Father with his prayer language out of any other place except his spirit. Did you know that when God gives you the gifts of the Holy Spirit, they flow out of the belly area and not the mind? The nine gifts of the Spirit all flow from your spirit area— the belly area.

The new man within you has to be boss—almost a tyrant. He has to have full control or there will be a wild man running around on the inside of you. When the spirit becomes king within you, the rest of you becomes a servant to the king. Then you are a spiritual entity just like Jesus. You will be living by a new man, new power, and new spirit. Your spiritual elements will surge up within you. You will start thinking, not from your mind, but from your spirit. Your emotions will not flare up and run away with you.

Did you know that millions of Christians have no idea whether or not they are living in the spirit? Did you know that every church problem that has ever been was born in the soulish part of the church, through the Adamic nature and not Jesus? We must learn to have the mind of Christ. The mind of Christ is a spiritual mind, not a carnal mind. Even as a Christian, you can still live with a carnal mind if you desire. In that case, however, your rewards in heaven will not be great.

Leave No Place for the Devil

When we lived in Manila, Philippines, one of their movie idols was converted. He had had a stroke. His tongue hung out the side of his mouth, and he was almost an idiot. They brought him to our services where Brother Clifton Erickson was the evangelist. God miraculously healed that man. His tongue went back into his mouth. He got up and began to talk. They brought him in a wheelchair, but he walked out of there while someone else pushed the chair. God had totally healed him. I went to his house to see him. His beautiful wife said to me, "Brother Sumrall, this is not the first time he has had this. He gets this way through his temper. I've seen him scream until he foams at the mouth and falls on the floor." I turned to Carlos and said, "That is your natural Adamic nature. If you ever do it again, you may die." He said, "I promise not to." He was dead in a month's time. His wife said, "Brother Sumrall, he was so angry and screamed so loudly that people could hear him a city block away. The very moment that he dropped dead, he was bellowing like a bull and cursing as loud as he could curse."

If you do not control that Adamic nature and subdue it with the power of the Spirit, it will ruin you and send you to the wrong place.

4
The Human Personality

◆◆◆

Until a Christian can differentiate between when the soul and spirit function and operate through him, he will continue to gravitate toward the lower life. He will not be able to rise in the spirit until he understands it. That is why it is so essential to know what is spirit. It is impossible to constantly walk in the spirit if you do not even know what the spirit is. The apostle Paul said in Galatians 5:16, *"This I say then, Walk in the Spirit, and ye shall not fulfil the lust of the flesh."* By walking in the Spirit, he meant walking in God, love, and holiness—not walking in darkness, sin, and rebellion toward God or your fellowman.

The Holy Spirit Energizes the Spirit-Man

"But if the Spirit of him that raised up Jesus from the dead dwell in you, he that raised up Christ from the dead shall also quicken your mortal bodies by his Spirit that dwelleth in you" (Romans 8:11). The Spirit that raised Jesus from the dead is the same power that comes to energize you in your spiritual parts. You are going to be quickened while you are living in your mortal body, not just in eternity.

"For to one is given by the Spirit the word of wisdom; to another the word of knowledge by the same Spirit" (1

Corinthians 12:8). These are two of the nine spiritual gifts from God. They never come through your mind, emotions, will, or your soulical parts.

Your Fruit Betrays You

In Galatians 5:22–23, Paul described the fruit of the spirit. This spirit is the born-again nature God has put within you. That spirit within you (separate from the soul) gives birth to these things. The first fruit Paul mentioned is love. Therefore, you have to ask yourself, "Am I living in love?" If you are, the fruit of your human spirit flowing out of your total being is love. When love does not flow from your being, then you are living in your soul. You know the activities of the spirit by love—if it is hate, or criticism, then it is Adamic. You will die spiritually if you are living in your Adamic nature. You will crush this newborn thing that God has put within you.

Next, the Word of God says the fruit of the spirit is joy. It is very saddening to find so many Christians who are really not happy. They will tell you that they are not happy. This is a problem resulting from their Adamic nature.

Now the fruit of the spirit-life is joy. God wants us to be happy. When you live by your feelings, every little thing that doesn't suit you makes you unhappy; then you're just living for the Adamic nature. If you do not live by Adam, you live by Christ.

Next he listed peace. Peace comes by being turned on positively, spiritually, and having an appreciation for your fellowman. It just does not come up the other way.

Romans 14:17 says that the kingdom of God is God's righteousness, which is the blood of Jesus Christ shed for you. It is peace and joy in the Holy Spirit. When you are born again by the Spirit of God and your spirit comes alive, it produces righteousness—God's righteousness. His righteousness covers you, and you become right with God, your fellowman, and yourself. When you become right, you become peaceful. If you are disturbed, nervous, and fearful all the time, you are living in your Adamic nature. You are not living by your spirit-man.

Paul went on to list several other attributes of the born-again spirit, including such fruit as longsuffering, gentleness, goodness, and faith.

5
Unity and Identity

We read in 1 John 5:7, *"For there are three that bear record in heaven, the Father, the Word, and the Holy Ghost: and these three are one."* Man is made, just like the Godhead, of three mighty dimensions. Each is distinct and different. The human structure is actually unique in all the creation and movements of God throughout the universe. In this creature called man we have the apex of His creation. We have something completely unique, because man does not have to serve God. Animals have to serve their masters. You can put a lion in a cage, and he cannot do a thing about it. God placed man here to make decisions and create his own destiny. God wants love, and you cannot love unless you have freedom. Prisoners do not have the chance to decide whom they love. Free men can choose whom and what they love. God made man unique in this way.

Made in God's Image

Man has a corporeal body. Beyond that, man possesses a dominant self that is his soul. The soul is distinct and different from the corporeal body. It is powerful. It leads, and it guides. The soul is a tremendous structure. Born-again people have a tremendous life, force, and ability called the spirit. Why is a man a threefold being, and not four, six, eight, or two? Man is made threefold in every dimension you find him. He is threefold because three is the number of God's divine perfection.

God made man first as a spirit. We are spirit. God is a spirit without corporeality. Demons are spirits without corporeality, or a physical being. Man is a spirit who possesses a soul and a body. God made man's spirit to be a king—not a slave. God made man's spirit to rule his triune personality. The spirit of man must rule; otherwise, the soul and the body will take over. They will become kings ruling in their own domain. This would cause the ruin of that personality and alienate it from God and happiness.

When a five-, six-, or seven-year-old child is led into a spiritual experience, he lives his whole life as a three-part being. What a pity it is for a man to live fifty years, then get saved, and say, "Oh, look how I wasted those fifty years living in the soul and the body—unhappy, miserable, when I could have been living on three." That is the reason we should win children to the Lord Jesus Christ. That is the reason the Bible says in Proverbs 22:6, *"Train up a child in the way he should go: and when he is old, he will not depart from it."* Get him born again. Get the blessing of God in him. Get the anointing of the Lord on him. Let him know what it means to live in the triune. Let him know that he is threefold, not two or one. Let him know the unity of his spirit, soul, and body, the three elements of the human personality. They can be like a symphony in their movements of loveliness, beauty, and music. They can be harmonious without distractions and broken hearts.

Man Was Created to Worship

In our worship the spirit can be adoring, praising, and magnifying God, just like the angels before the throne of God in heaven. At that precise moment the soul or the mind can be thinking of the beauties of heaven, and of all the wonderful things that come to us through Christ. The emotions that belong to the soul can be in a state of ecstasy with joy flowing at a higher level than it does regularly. The will can be in divine submission to and perfect rhythm with God. It can be harmonizing the spirit and soul with the will, saying, "I like this. I want this. I'm for this." While the soul and spirit are worshipping God, the body can have the expressions of worship. The head and hands may be lifted in adoration and worship. The eyes can have the light of heaven in them. The lips can be singing the praises of God. In this way the total human personality is involved in worship.

How many worship services do you attend where you find that the three parts of you are not fully functioning? The mind is wandering off on what is going on next week. The spirit has no part in the effort. However, if you are going to have the perfect man—the ideal person—there has to be unity and identity. The spirit is doing its function, the soulical part its function, and the bodily parts their functions. The three are there, but they are united.

Divinity Operates as One

We must realize that we are created exactly as God in heaven. The same thing exists in heaven. The Father, Son, and Holy Spirit, together in the majestic throne room of God, decided to make man in their own image.

This was the movement not of one but of all of them. *"God said, Let us make man in our image"* (Genesis 1:26). God said, *"after **our** likeness"* (emphasis added). Here we see the flowing of more than one.

"He saw the Spirit of God descending like a dove, and lighting upon him: and lo a voice from heaven, saying, This is my beloved Son, in whom I am well pleased" (Matthew 3:16–17). Here the divine trinity is functioning and operating in divine action. Christ was being baptized in the river Jordan. The Father was speaking from heaven. The Holy Spirit was descending to anoint and to bless the Son as He went forth on His journey through life and upon His occupation on this earth.

The divine Trinity made man triune. *"And the very God of peace sanctify you wholly; and I pray God your whole spirit and soul and body be preserved blameless unto the coming of our Lord Jesus Christ"* (1 Thessalonians 5:23). We see that the born-again person possesses the same component parts that Adam possessed before he fell in the Garden of Eden. We have been reinstated.

Man's Threefold Personality

The personality of man is so closely knit that it takes the all-powerful Word of God to divide the soul from the spirit. Man cannot do it. Science will never figure it out. Philosophy will never know what it is. They will never have the answers to the reality of what makes a man a spirit, what his soul does, and how it functions within him.

The Body

Almighty God fashioned the human body from the clay of the earth. *"And the Lord God formed man of the dust of the ground, and breathed into his nostrils the breath of life; and man became a living soul"* (Genesis 2:7). Originally there was a close kinship between man and his environment. God did not use dust from the moon to make a man here on the earth. His outer shell is like the earth, the area in which he lives and exists.

The body is easy for us to classify and identify. Its five senses (seeing, feeling, smelling, touching, and hearing) are ever with us. We see that the earthly part of us was created to serve us as a servant, even as a slave. The mortal part of man, the slave, was created to obey his spirit part. If the inward man is evil, the carnal, clay man will manifest all the evils of the inward man. If you have lust inside you, and if you want to hear every dirty thing you can because there is a spirit of lust within you, that spirit will manifest itself through the clay man. If the inner man is spiritual, the body will demonstrate the fruit of the Spirit. It will be exactly what the spirit wants it to be. It is the outer shell—the human body.

The Soul

Inside the human shell you have the soulish or Adamic man. It is full of unspeakable mysteries. Maybe science on this earth will never understand the intricacies of the intellect, emotion, and willpower that combine to make your soul. This part of man is real self-life, with a close relationship with the outside shell of the body. Your mind, emotions, and will live skin-deep, close to the outside of your body. The soul with its three areas helps the body to know what to do, when to do it, and how to do it. God joined the body and soul together with His breath. He breathed into Adam and made the mind, emotions, will, and flesh come alive.

He breathed upon them, and the two areas flowed together to be subservient to a further deeper area. Man's body and soul can be good or bad in relationship to the third area, his spirit—his born-again nature.

Inside the clay house is a soul. Beyond the soul we find man's spirit. This spirit is as distinct as the other two areas. It is as different as darkness is from light. God gave man's spirit the propensities of communication and communion with deity that do not belong to man otherwise. Your mind cannot reach deity. If it could, the philosophers would have all of it, and uneducated people would have none of it. God said in 1 Corinthians 1:21, *"The world by wisdom knew not God."*

The Spirit

In his spirit area, man was created to be able to communicate with the divine world. Through your spirit you can communicate with God. The reason sinners say all kinds of funny things about Christians is that they do not live in the same world. For sinners, looking at a Christian is like looking into a barrel that is all sealed up and has one little hole. They are on the outside trying to look in and they cannot see a thing, but if you get on the inside you can see everything by looking out. That is how it is when the spirit rules within you. God gave man this spirit. He gave him a spirit structure so that he might understand and know things about God, eternity, and himself.

There Is Power in Unity

In the perfect man we see three things. As a body he walks, eats, sees, hears, and feels. He has the five senses God gave him. With his soulical parts, he has power over all the animals of the earth. He has power over all the things that live and the vegetation of the earth. Through his soulical parts, he rules the natural things that are around him. He possesses emotions to admire the sunrise, which an animal does not; to admire the sunset, which a beast cannot; to feel real affection and love toward another. He has the willpower to choose to walk as a king on the face of the earth. When he walks in his physical, soulical, and spiritual parts, then he walks with divinity—with God, not with animals and other men. Adam walked with the Most High God. With his spirit he understood his limitations, what he should do and what he should not do, relative to good and evil. In man's triunity he has a king, a servant, and a slave within him; all three are meshed into one being.

The spirit must exercise his kingship by praising God. Praise brings you into direct relationship with God. If you never lift up your voice and praise God, then fellowship with God cannot exist. In church we should sing joyfully unto the Lord. I have heard heathens sing all over the world, and there was not a joyful note. It is mournful; it is death. I have heard the Muslims as they pray over loudspeakers all over their lands. It is sad and depressing.

Let the Spirit Be King

The Word of God says, "Let the people rejoice!" (See Psalm 97:1.) The beginning of your walk with God is to be sure that your spirit is king. It is your relationship with the Most High. It is your relationship with peace. It is your relationship with joy. It is your divine relationship. Bring your spirit into focus as the supreme leader of your life by reading the Word, praying, and worshipping.

God made man's soul to be a servant. Make your mind your servant, not your lord. Make your emotions your servant. God did not make your emotions for you to get up every morning and say, "How do I feel?" Through your spirit, you are to tell your emotions how to feel. Say, "Emotions, it is time to rejoice!" David said to his soul in Psalm 42:5, *"Why art thou cast down, O my soul? and why art thou disquieted in me? hope thou in God."* The spirit David was speaking to the soul David, saying, "Rejoice in the Lord." He commanded himself to rejoice in the Lord. Millions and millions of people make their emotions king and live by them. That is the reason for divorces, heartaches, troubles, and all kinds of sorrows. Millions live in their Adamic, soulical nature, rather than by the spirit nature and by the Spirit and power of God. God helps us to live resourcefully, gloriously, and wonderfully as a united man with a king, servant, and slave living together in one house— your body. In that house, you must know who is lord— the spirit made alive by Jesus. As you walk, talk, and sing to Him, your soulical parts must obey and your physical parts must respond and say, "Yes, I obey."

I ask you to examine yourself and say, "Lord, I am going to make Jesus the King of my life. He's going to put His Spirit in me to guide my life in every way."

6
The Mystery of the Human Body

◆◆◆

*T*he Homo sapiens species has exhausted the imaginations of a million artists during the past six thousand years. These masters have painted man's muscles, the contour of his face, and the light in his eyes. From his toes to his hair, nothing has escaped the keen eye of the artist. Yet the perfect portrait of the human remains to be completed.

The human body has puzzled doctors. Every day scientists discover more truth about the human body.

The human body has mystified the philosopher in the classroom. The faces, the languages, and the cultures of the earth challenge his ingenuity.

A few years ago, chemists said that the value of the human body was about ninety-eight cents. They were estimating the value of the iron, zinc, and minerals in the human body. However, modern science says man's body is worth a million dollars!

Using a chemical supply catalog, a professor of the University of Washington recently calculated the value of the marketable substances in a normal one-hundred-and-fifty-pound man. At today's prices, for example, the body's ten thousand units of the clotting agent prothrobin would sell for $30,600. The forty grams of myoglobin, another blood component, are worth $100,000. The professor said, "I've always been kind of appalled at the people who sell their plasma for only $10 a pint, when in that pint you have maybe thirty grams of albumin—which is worth $945."

God says that your human body is worth all the riches of planet Earth. *"For what is a man profited, if he shall gain the whole world, and lose his own soul? or what shall a man give in exchange for his soul?"* (Matthew 16:26).

Agility of the Human Body

The agility of the human body makes it possible for man to skate on ice, jump high in the air, run like the wind, ride in space, or go to the depths of the ocean in a submarine.

The human body has fingers that can dance on a piano keyboard or strum a guitar. It has lungs that can blow a wind instrument to make beautiful music. The human body is capable of building houses, planes, cars, and scientific instruments.

Famous Bodies: "The Body Beautiful"

Since time immemorial humans have admired the male and female physique. The mighty muscles of Atlas carrying the world are an exclamation of the strength and magnificence of the human form. The famous Pieta in Rome, with Mary holding Jesus, is a symphony in stone.

In the Bible, God tells of the strongest man in history, Samson.

And Samson lay till midnight, and arose at midnight, and took the doors of the gate of the city, and the two posts, and went away with them, bar and all, and put

*them upon his shoulders, and carried them up to the
top of an hill that is before Hebron.*   (Judges 16:3)

Those heavy city gates, wide enough for chariots and
horses to pass through, possibly covered with metal to
hold back the enemy in the time of war, were ripped
off their hinges by naked hands. He placed them on his
shoulders and carried them up a Judean hill. What a
sight to behold! What a body!

Feminine bodies have been commercialized from
Jezebel, who tried to kill Elijah, to Herodias, who had
John the Baptist beheaded, and Cleopatra, who used her
body allurements to capture the hearts of emperors.

The Bible describes the legendary monstrosity
Goliath, the Philistine giant, in 1 Samuel 17:4: *"And there
went out a champion out of the camp of the Philistines, named
Goliath, of Gath, whose height was six cubits and a span."*
Finis J. Dake said six cubits measured thirteen feet, four
inches. Imagine seeing a human standing over thirteen
feet tall!

The Bible says that there was a family of these
giants.

> *And it came to pass after this, that there was again a
> battle with the Philistines at Gob: then Sibbechai the
> Hushathite slew Saph, which was of the sons of the
> giant. And there was again a battle in Gob with the
> Philistines, where Elhanan the son of Jaareoregim, a
> Bethlehemite, slew the brother of Goliath the Gittite,
> the staff of whose spear was like a weaver's beam. And
> there was yet a battle in Gath, where was a man of
> great stature, that had on every hand six fingers, and
> on every foot six toes, four and twenty in number; and
> he also was born to the giant. And when he defied
> Israel, Jonathan the son of Shimeah the brother of
> David slew him. These four were born to the giant in*

> Gath, and fell by the hand of David, and by the hand
> of his servants.   (2 Samuel 21:18–22)

The Human Body Is a House of Five Rooms

For six thousand years of human history, one of man's greatest astonishments has been the human body. Almost daily, science discovers something new about the amazing operations of the human body. This is because the human body was created by the Most High God. It forever remains the most mysterious of all creations.

Man must not forget that his physical body is important! God designed the contours of his outer person. God gave man five senses that live together in the house called the body.

Your eyes watch where you are going and receive information for the brain. This is the room of sight. Much delightful living comes to us through the miracle of sight. The flowers, stars, and oceans thrill the human mind through the joy of sight.

Your ears hear the voices and the audio vibrations of planet Earth. There are the sweet sounds of a baby's laughter and bitter sounds of war and hate. Much of man's living is in this room.

The smell of delicious food being prepared and exotic flowers fills the air around us. The body delights itself with the stimulating aromas of planet Earth. Once I visited a perfume factory where there were hundreds of exotic scents from all over the world. It was impossible to decide on the sweetest fragrance.

Touch is so marvelous. Our sense of touch feels the majesty of God's creation. The touch of water running over the body, the touch of a baby's skin, and the touch of a gorgeous flower are all part of the wonderful room of feeling.

There is a delightful world of delicious *tastes* for men to enjoy. Your ability to taste gives a million flavors to vibrant living.

The Power Plant of the Human Body

God designed the most remarkable pump and placed it in your chest. It is called the heart. It is a veritable miracle! It works harder and longer than any engine ever made by man.

There is also the majesty of the human brain. The Most High God designed it and placed it in your head. It is far beyond medical comprehension. It is now known that this computer of the brain holds billions of pieces of information on its "microchips" and "floppy discs."

To all this, the Bible simply says that man is fearfully and wonderfully made. *"I will praise thee; for I am fearfully and wonderfully made: marvellous are thy works; and that my soul knoweth right well"* (Psalm 139:14).

The Human Body Did Not Evolve

God, the Sovereign of the universe, in His eternal wisdom conceived the desire to create an intellectual, moral, and physical earth-creature with spiritual responsibility and integrity. He made him to express His own nature of love so He could receive love from man.

Man is the most intricate of all the original creations God created. Even at this moment, man is a labyrinth of mystery and beauty.

And God said, Let us make man in our image, after our likeness: and let them have dominion over the fish

*of the sea, and over the fowl of the air, and over the
cattle, and over all the earth, and over every creeping
thing that creepeth upon the earth. So God created
man in his own image, in the image of God created
he him; male and female created he them. And God
blessed them, and God said unto them, Be fruitful,
and multiply, and replenish the earth, and subdue it:
and have dominion over the fish of the sea, and over
the fowl of the air, and over every living thing that
moveth upon the earth.* (Genesis 1:26–28)

*And the LORD God formed man of the dust of the
ground, and breathed into his nostrils the breath of
life; and man became a living soul.* (Genesis 2:7)

Man did not slowly evolve by the power of fortu-
itous forces. Man did not arrive on earth by accident. In
truth, he is fearfully and wonderfully made to the fullest meaning of those human expressions.

The Human Body out of Control

Since the fall of man in the Garden of Eden, the
human body and its lusts have created sorrow and pain
for man.

For example David, king of Israel, has been mocked
for three thousand years because of his affair with
Bathsheba. David's bodily transgression has caused
much of his greatness to be forgotten. He was a great
warrior. He was a mighty king for forty years. He composed some of the earth's most beautiful songs.

The uncontrolled body of Samson has made him
a laughingstock for generations. Today films are made
about Samson and Delilah.

The human body made wise King Solomon a fool.
The Bible says he had a thousand wives and concubines.

They finally took his heart away from God. We read in 1 Kings 11:1–13,

> *But king Solomon loved many strange women, together with the daughter of Pharaoh, women of the Moabites, Ammonites, Edomites, Zidonians, and Hittites; of the nations concerning which the LORD said unto the children of Israel, Ye shall not go in to them, neither shall they come in unto you: for surely they will turn away your heart after their gods: Solomon clave unto these in love. And he had seven hundred wives, princesses, and three hundred concubines: and his wives turned away his heart. For it came to pass, when Solomon was old, that his wives turned away his heart after other gods: and his heart was not perfect with the LORD his God, as was the heart of David his father. For Solomon went after Ashtoreth the goddess of the Zidonians, and after Milcom the abomination of the Ammonites. And Solomon did evil in the sight of the LORD, and went not fully after the LORD, as did David his father. Then did Solomon build an high place for Chemosh, the abomination of Moab, in the hill that is before Jerusalem, and for Molech, the abomination of the children of Ammon. And likewise did he for all his strange wives, which burnt incense and sacrificed unto their gods. And the LORD was angry with Solomon, because his heart was turned from the LORD God of Israel, which had appeared unto him twice, and had commanded him concerning this thing, that he should not go after other gods: but he kept not that which the LORD commanded. Wherefore the LORD said unto Solomon, Forasmuch as this is done of thee, and thou hast not kept my covenant and my statutes, which I have commanded thee, I will surely rend the kingdom from thee, and will give it to thy servant. Notwithstanding in thy days I will not do it for David thy father's sake: but I will rend it*

> out of the hand of thy son. Howbeit I will not rend
> away all the kingdom; but will give one tribe to thy
> son for David my servant's sake, and for Jerusalem's
> sake which I have chosen.

So the intellectually wisest man of history permitted his body, the lowest part of his person, to rule him. Living by sinful flesh almost destroyed his eternal destiny.

Man Must Learn That the Body Is More

> Therefore I say unto you, Take no thought for your
> life, what ye shall eat, or what ye shall drink; nor yet
> for your body, what ye shall put on. Is not the life
> more than meat, and the body than raiment?
> (Matthew 6:25)

The Body Is the Temple of God

> Know ye not that ye are the temple of God, and that the
> Spirit of God dwelleth in you?   (1 Corinthians 3:16)

> And what agreement hath the temple of God with
> idols? for ye are the temple of the living God; as God
> hath said, I will dwell in them, and walk in them; and
> I will be their God, and they shall be my people.
> (2 Corinthians 6:16)

What a house! What excitement!

Keep the House

God made man responsible for his own body. God said it is better to lose parts of the body than for the total person to be lost.

And if thy right eye offend thee, pluck it out, and cast it from thee: for it is profitable for thee that one of thy members should perish, and not that thy whole body should be cast into hell. (Matthew 5:29)

And fear not them which kill the body, but are not able to kill the soul: but rather fear him which is able to destroy both soul and body in hell. (Matthew 10:28)

Paul addressed all Christians in 1 Corinthians 9:27, *"But I keep under my body, and bring it into subjection: lest that by any means, when I have preached to others, I myself should be a castaway."* This is a word of caution to all of us.

Satan Wants the Human Body

The Bible says there are three enemies of the body:
1. The world
2. The flesh
3. The devil

Love not the world, neither the things that are in the world. If any man love the world, the love of the Father is not in him. For all that is in the world, the lust of the flesh, and the lust of the eyes, and the pride of life, is not of the Father, but is of the world. And the world passeth away, and the lust thereof: but he that doeth the will of God abideth for ever. (1 John 2:15–17)

"But chiefly them that walk after the flesh in the lust of uncleanness, and despise government. Presumptuous are they, selfwilled, they are not afraid to speak evil of dignities" (2 Peter 2:10). When the flesh yields to these distractions, it cannot please God, who created it.

The devil wants to take the movements of the human body and distort them. The devil desires lust to leer from the human eye. The devil wants man to scream with his voice in hate and violence. The devil wants men and women to hear the obscene and demonic. I have personally witnessed the human body twisted by sin—the alcoholic, the drug addict, and the sex deviant.

Sickness also twists and destroys the human body. Rheumatoid arthritis, carnivorous cancer, and deterioration of the mind until the victims are locked away like criminals, are all examples of the terrible attacks of Satan. Those who yield to the occult, spiritism, oriental gurus, and mantras become so controlled that they find it impossible to shake off the bondage. This bondage can totally warp the mind and body God created for His glory. I have also witnessed the body suffering from the lusts of the soul. The body is a servant of the soul. It can become a slave to the mind, emotions, and will. The body is a real photograph of your soulical being. It has to obey the soulical powers of mind, emotion, and will. It can revolt unto death, but in life the body carries out all the manifestations of the human soul.

7
The Fall of the Human Body

◆●◆

A dam must have been magnificent when he rose up from the earth, made alive by the breath of Elohim, the Creator-God.

God, with His fingers, had shaped him, designed him, and created his internal organs to function.

God breathed upon His creation of red earth, Adam, and infused His Spirit within him. What a mixture of divinity and dust! Elohim liked the results.

Adam did not learn to walk or talk; he immediately walked and talked with God. Then God further surrounded Adam with a covering of the same Shekinah glory that covers His majesty. Adam was beautiful. God made him the king of all His creation.

> And God said, Let us make man in our image, after our likeness: and let them have dominion over the fish of the sea, and over the fowl of the air, and over the cattle, and over all the earth, and over every creeping thing that creepeth upon the earth. (Genesis 1:26)

There was no evolution. On the other hand, since the time of man's rebellion against God, there has been a state of devolution.

Adam's Pristine Glory

Adam walked and talked with God in his human body. The human body was originally created to live forever. At his fall into transgression, Adam's body, along with other parts of the original person, suffered great change.

Adam's body lost its covering in the Garden of Eden. God in His love and mercy made garments of skin for the human body.

After the Fall, the human body changed. It became weary and sick. It came to know death.

In the Fall, Adam lost his communion with God and one-third of him died. *"And he said, I heard thy voice in the garden, and I was afraid, because I was naked; and I hid myself"* (Genesis 3:10). God said Adam would die the day he sinned. Adam's body and soul did not die, but his spirit ceased to enjoy a relationship with God.

Adam's Total Rebellion

Because God created in Adam the power of deliberate action, he could obey God or rebel. The sin of Adam was volitional.

Adam was created in the image and likeness of God.

> And it came to pass in the sixth year, in the sixth month, in the fifth day of the month, as I sat in mine house, and the elders of Judah sat before me, that the hand of the Lord GOD fell there upon me. Then I beheld, and lo a likeness as the appearance of fire: from the appearance of his loins even downward, fire; and from his loins even upward, as the appearance of brightness, as the colour of amber.   (Ezekiel 8:1–2)

Jehovah is clothed with fire that does not consume. Adam was clothed the same way.

The pristine clothing of Adam was the same as the burning bush when the Lord appeared unto Moses.

> *Now Moses kept the flock of Jethro his father in law, the priest of Midian: and he led the flock to the backside of the desert, and came to the mountain of God, even to Horeb. And the angel of the LORD appeared unto him in a flame of fire out of the midst of a bush: and he looked, and, behold, the bush burned with fire, and the bush was not consumed.* (Exodus 3:1–2)

Adam and Eve must have been beautiful.

The Human Body without God

Since the day of Adam's transgression, man, away from God, has lived by the works of human flesh.

> *Now the works of the flesh are manifest, which are these; adultery, fornication, uncleanness, lasciviousness, idolatry, witchcraft, hatred, variance, emulations, wrath, strife, seditions, heresies, envyings, murders, drunkenness, revellings, and such like.* (Galatians 5:19–21)

Adam walked out of Eden with Eve, his wife. They were devastated losers. Now they had only two parts functioning—soul and body. They had lost their identity as triune beings. Neither Adam nor his seed were now the total man.

8

What Man Must Do with His Human Body

◆●●

I beseech you therefore, brethren, by the mercies of God, that ye present your bodies a living sacrifice, holy, acceptable unto God, which is your reasonable service. And be not conformed to this world: but be ye transformed by the renewing of your mind, that ye may prove what is that good, and acceptable, and perfect, will of God. (Romans 12:1–2)

The Homo sapiens species is body-conscious. Man's body is his corporeal presence. It is the nearest entity to him. He washes it. He clothes it. He feels it. Sometimes he abuses it!

Jesus' first attack from Satan was against His body. *"Make this stone bread"* (Luke 4:3). The tempter recognized that Christ possessed such power, but the Spirit of Christ controlled His body. By the use of the Word of God, *"Man does not live by bread alone"* (Luke 4:4), Jesus destroyed Satan's attack against His body.

Christ, at all times, taught against self-gratification. Some people live only to gratify the desires of the human body. Jesus refused to do this.

The Human Body in Battle

Since time immemorial, rulers have penalized their captured prisoners by causing them to fight wild animals. The royal lions were kept to combat and devour humans. It is amazing that the Roman emperors demanded gladiators with their human bodies to engage in deadly combat with wild beasts. The human gladiators were forced to battle to the death against ferocious and hungry beasts. The Caesars and the noblemen of Rome applauded while carnivorous beasts tore men and women limb from limb.

Still today in several modern nations there are bullfights. *El Toreador* walks into the ring and fights *el toro,* the bull. Thousands of people watch and scream "Vive el toro" when the beast sinks his horns into the human body. It is sickening to watch a human body fight a wild animal.

In our own country many of today's sports are body contests. A human body on the football field is thrust with total impact against another body. In the wrestling ring, one huge body casts another human body against the canvas. In the boxing arena, it is one human body punishing another body with heavy blows.

This seems to be the eternal story regarding the human body: it is constantly mutilated by man or beast. The devil is the conceiver of such abuse. Surely, God never planned for the human body to be abused.

God's view of the human body, and the Bible, teach us that the human body is to be immortal.

> *Behold, I show you a mystery; we shall not all sleep, but we shall all be changed, in a moment, in the twinkling of an eye, at the last trump: for the trumpet shall sound, and the dead shall be raised incorruptible, and we shall be changed. For this corruptible must put on incorruption, and this mortal must put on immortality. So when this corruptible shall have*

> put on incorruption, and this mortal shall have put on
> immortality, then shall be brought to pass the saying
> that is written, Death is swallowed up in victory. O
> death, where is thy sting? O grave, where is thy vic-
> tory?   (1 Corinthians 15:51–55)

The body is a treasure in an earthen vessel. *"But we have this treasure in earthen vessels, that the excellency of the power may be of God, and not of us"* (2 Corinthians 4:7).

The human body is a member of Christ. The great apostle Paul revealed that the human body is actually a member of the body of Christ.

> *Know ye not that your bodies are the members of*
> *Christ? shall I then take the members of Christ, and*
> *make them the members of an harlot? God forbid.*
>   (1 Corinthians 6:15)

We must remember that it is not possible for the human body to be good and bad at the same time. When the members or senses of the body are members of Christ's body, they cannot be sold in the marketplace like a harlot selling her body.

The body you live in is not yours. *"What? know ye not that your body is the temple of the Holy Ghost which is in you, which ye have of God, and ye are not your own?"* (1 Corinthians 6:19). It is a tremendous fallacy to declare that your body is yours to misuse as you wish. Your body is a worship center or temple where Jehovah God is worshipped.

"For ye are bought with a price: therefore glorify God in your body, and in your spirit, which are God's" (1 Corinthians 6:20). We are purchased with the supreme price of Christ's own blood, and we are commanded to glorify God in this fleshly body.

The human body should not be disfigured. *"Ye shall not make any cuttings in your flesh for the dead, nor print any marks upon you: I am the L*ORD*"* (Leviticus 19:28). The heathen and some in our land make tattoos on their flesh. God demands that men not mutilate their skin.

Man should manifest Christ in his body. I do not believe many people recognize this great truth.

> *Always bearing about in the body the dying of the Lord Jesus, that the life also of Jesus might be made manifest in our body. For we which live are alway delivered unto death for Jesus' sake, that the life also of Jesus might be made manifest in our mortal flesh.*
> (2 Corinthians 4:10–11)

Our mortal bodies, redeemed by Christ's blood, are to manifest and reveal the nature of Jesus Christ in our mortal flesh.

God says that man must not permit sin to rule his mortal body. *"Let not sin therefore reign in your mortal body, that ye should obey it in the lusts thereof"* (Romans 6:12). Sin is rebellion and transgression against the law of God. It must not sit upon the throne of your life to rule and enslave you.

What God Wants You to Know about Your Body

God desires that you present your body as a living sacrifice. *"I beseech you therefore, brethren, by the mercies of God, that ye present your bodies a living sacrifice, holy, acceptable unto God, which is your reasonable service"* (Romans 12:1). This is not a dead sacrifice but a daily giving of your body and its five senses to Jehovah. It is a volitional action that God said was reasonable.

Man is required to bridle the body.

> *For in many things we offend all. If any man offend not in word, the same is a perfect man, and able also to bridle the whole body. Behold, we put bits in the horses' mouths, that they may obey us; and we turn about their whole body.*　　　　　(James 3:2)

Just as a horse or other animal has a bridle to make it obedient to its master, God says the human body must be bridled. The devil wants your body to be wild, untamed, rebellious, and Satan-oriented, but God says, *"Bridle the whole body."* This means hold your body in check the same way the rider holds his horse by a bridle in its tender mouth. God says this is the way of the perfect man.

Man will be judged by the deeds of the body. *"For we must all appear before the judgment seat of Christ; that every one may receive the things done in his body, according to that he hath done, whether it be good or bad"* (2 Corinthians 5:10). All human deeds done in this body must one day be judged by Christ at His judgment seat.

> *But why dost thou judge thy brother? or why dost thou set at nought thy brother? for we shall all stand before the judgment seat of Christ.*　　(Romans 14:10)

Man should manifest Christ in his body. Paul said in 2 Corinthians 4:10, *"Always bearing about in the body the dying of the Lord Jesus, that the life also of Jesus might be made manifest in our body."* What a privilege it is for the life of Christ to be manifested in the human body.

The human body was not created for moral uncleanness. *"Meats for the belly, and the belly for meats: but God shall destroy both it and them. Now the body is not for fornication, but for the Lord; and the Lord for the body"*

(1 Corinthians 6:13). God specifically warns the total human that the body is not for illicit sex. It is to be dedicated to God.

God demands that Christ be magnified in the human body. *"According to my earnest expectation and my hope, that in nothing I shall be ashamed, but that with all boldness, as always, so now also Christ shall be magnified in my body, whether it be by life, or by death"* (Philippians 1:20). The human body is to exalt Christ. The human body is to magnify or enlarge Christ as a magnifying glass enlarges print. It is to increase the image of Christ on this earth.

The body can be made blameless in Christ. *"And the very God of peace sanctify you wholly; and I pray God your whole spirit and soul and body be preserved blameless unto the coming of our Lord Jesus Christ"* (1 Thessalonians 5:23). The body is cleansed of all bodily transgressions through the power of the new birth. You become dead to sin, but very much alive in your spirit.

What Satan Wants You to Do with Your Body

The devil desires you to yield your body to him. The devil has always hated man's body because it is made in the image of God.

The first sin committed on earth was of the body. Eve first saw the forbidden fruit with her eyes, felt it with her hands, tasted it with her mouth, listened to the devil with her ears, and surrendered her total person to Satan.

The devil desires to make the body sick. Sickness is a limited death. He wishes to bring pain, injury, and physical death to all mankind.

The devil would like your body to be unclean. *"Wherefore God also gave them up to uncleanness through* the lusts of their own hearts, to dishonour their own bodies between themselves" (Romans 1:24).

If the human person obeys the devil, his body will be unclean morally, spiritually, and physically. The devil is unclean. Some of his demons are called "unclean spirits." *"For he said unto him, Come out of the man, thou unclean spirit"* (Mark 5:8).

The devil would like to destroy your body prematurely.

> *Lord, have mercy on my son: for he is a lunatic, and sore vexed: for ofttimes he falleth into the fire, and oft into the water. And I brought him to thy disciples, and they could not cure him. Then Jesus answered and said, O faithless and perverse generation, how long shall I be with you? how long shall I suffer you? bring him hither to me. And Jesus rebuked the devil; and he departed out of him: and the child was cured from that very hour.* (Matthew 17:15–18)

The devil told Jesus to jump off the pinnacle of the temple.

> *Then the devil taketh him up into the holy city, and setteth him on a pinnacle of the temple, and saith unto him, If thou be the Son of God, cast thyself down: for it is written, He shall give his angels charge concerning thee: and in their hands they shall bear thee up, lest at any time thou dash thy foot against a stone. Jesus said unto him, It is written again, Thou shalt not tempt the Lord thy God.* (Matthew 4:5–7)

What a glorious rebuff to Satan.

We have an account of how Satan tormented a young man into mutilating his own body.

And they came over unto the other side of the sea, into the country of the Gadarenes. And when he was come out of the ship, immediately there met him out of the tombs a man with an unclean spirit, who had his dwelling among the tombs; and no man could bind him, no, not with chains: because that he had been often bound with fetters and chains, and the chains had been plucked asunder by him, and the fetters broken in pieces: neither could any man tame him. And always, night and day, he was in the mountains, and in the tombs, crying, and cutting himself with stones. (Mark 5:1–5)

Man must either obey God or the devil with his human body. The human body can be in the image and likeness of God or the image and likeness of Satan. Decide for God.

9
The Human Body of Jesus

◆◆◆

When studying the remarkable human body of man, it is necessary to consider the human body of the Lord Jesus Christ. Many people in our generation do not understand either the importance of the human body or, possibly, what the Bible says about the human body. In this chapter, we will try to particularly understand the human body of Jesus.

Soulical Parts

Most of us have studied man's mind, emotions, and will. However, we often stop there and do not realize the importance of the human body. *"In the beginning was the Word"* (John 1:1). This *logos,* or living Word, was the beginning of everything. Whatever was in existence had the living Word.

Who are God and Jesus? What do God and Jesus look like? A word is an expression and fulfillment of a thought. It is the bringing forth of a thought so that others might see it and understand it. Jesus Christ is the total expression of God. The Word was with God...*Elohim.* The Word was with God, the Maker. The Word was God. In verse fourteen, *"And the Word was made flesh."*

These are the most dynamic words ever spoken by human lips. That which was eternal and creative was made flesh. *"And the Word was made flesh, and dwelt among us, (and we beheld his glory, the glory as of the only begotten of the Father,) full of grace and truth"* (John 1:14).

It is amazing that divinity and humanity ever collaborated and became joined together as one. Actual divinity was housed in a human body. How amazing! How remarkable! How wonderful!

A Prepared Body

Christ's human body came to this earth by God's preparation. *"Wherefore when he cometh into the world, he saith, Sacrifice and offering thou wouldest not, but a body hast thou prepared me"* (Hebrews 10:5). The body was prepared by the eternal Father. The Word says that God no longer desires a sacrifice of goats, lambs, or doves for the remission of sins. God prepared a body that is accepted by Him as a sacrifice and offering for the remission of all sins. It was a prepared body. It was a prophetic body. It knew that it was coming before it came. In Genesis 3:15, God prophesied, *"And I will put enmity between thee and the woman, and between thy seed and her seed; it shall bruise thy head, and thou shalt bruise his heel."* There was to be a battle between the Seed of the woman and Satan. Though you and I are the seed of the woman, the true Seed of the woman was the body called Jesus.

The Lord Jesus Christ came as the final expression of that Seed. "He shall bruise thy head, and thou shalt bruise His heel." Here is the first promise. The first promise had to do with a body. The Seed of the woman was to be a human body. The first prophecy ever given from heaven was the promise of a body that would be born one day from a woman, just like any other man. A human body would bruise the head of the devil. That body would accept the hurt of a heel. It was prophesied by God in Genesis and again in Isaiah 7:14, *"Therefore the Lord himself shall give you a sign; Behold, a virgin shall conceive, and bear a son, and shall call his name Immanuel."* Seven hundred years before the body came to this earth, it was prophesied that a girl who had never been married, or known a man, would in a miraculous way conceive. A sperm, by the power of the Holy Spirit, would enter into her and she would bring forth a son. His name would be called Immanuel, "God with us." This prophetic Seed of human flesh and blood was manifested when Jesus Christ was born in Bethlehem.

His Body Was Just like Ours

A human body came from heaven, yet that human body was like your body. *"And she brought forth her first-born son, and wrapped him in swaddling clothes, and laid him in a manger; because there was no room for them in the inn"* (Luke 2:7). During conception something very minute was placed within this woman. It grew, matured, and changed and was born as a seventeen- or eighteen-inch baby. After birth it increased in stature. Jesus had human flesh, blood, and bone.

This prophesied seed came to save the human race. Hebrews 10:10 says, *"By the which will we are sanctified through the offering of the body of Jesus Christ once for all."* We are sanctified. The human body of Jesus was offered to God for our sins. His human body, the Bible says, was offered once and for all. It cannot be offered every Sunday. He was offered one time forever and never needs to be offered again.

His Coming Was a Miracle

The body of Jesus was the greatest miracle ever performed on the face of this earth. God was able to slip His Son into a little cell, place Him into a woman like He promised four thousand years before in the Garden of Eden, and bring forth the Savior of the world for all. John 3:16 says God, *Elohim God,* loved the world—not the geographical world, but the world of hurts, problems, sorrows, and depressions. God loved the world so much that He found a means by which He could bring us His only begotten Son, who had been with Him forever and forever. So *"whosoever believeth in him should not perish, but have everlasting life."* The greatest miracle took place when this Son of God entered the human family and said, "I will be the promised Seed from Genesis to bring reconciliation between God the Father and people to save the human race."

"Who his own self bare our sins in his own body on the tree, that we, being dead to sins, should live unto righteousness: by whose stripes ye were healed" (1 Peter 2:24). Christ's body is the only avenue to eternal life. The Bible says, *"His own self bare our sins in his own body."* You are healed by His flesh. I do not think we have begun to realize what we can do in our flesh for God. We have always downgraded the flesh and called it bad names, but the flesh can be spiritual. The flesh can walk in holiness and dress right. The flesh can talk right. God would like us to dedicate our bodies to Him.

> *I beseech you therefore, brethren, by the mercies of God, that ye present your bodies a living sacrifice, holy, acceptable unto God, which is your reasonable service. And be not conformed to this world: but be ye transformed by the renewing of your mind, that ye*

may prove what is that good, and acceptable, and per-
fect, will of God.   (Romans 12:1–2)

It is easy to offer God a dead sacrifice. Some of you say, "When I die I am going to give so much money to God." If you have something to give to your kids, you should give it to them while you are alive. You might want to see how they use it. If you have something to give to God, give it to Him now. The Bible says you are going to be judged by the deeds done in the body, not in the spirit.

Eternal Life Is Related to His Body

"Then Jesus said unto them, Verily, verily, I say unto you, except ye eat the flesh of the Son of man, and drink his blood, ye have no life in you" (John 6:53). Your salvation is related to His body—His flesh and blood. The Bible says the life of the flesh is in the blood. The life He had in His flesh was His blood that flowed through Him. If you want to live forever, you must partake of His flesh. Unless you eat of that flesh and drink of that blood, you will never have eternal life.

"Jesus saith unto him, I am the way, the truth, and the life: no man cometh unto the Father, but by me" (John 14:6). If you go to the Father, there is only one way to go. That way is by the person who lived in Nazareth, Galilee, and Judea; who healed and blessed the people of that time. In His body He blessed them and helped them. He is God's way, God's truth, and God's life.

"Whoso eateth my flesh, and drinketh my blood, hath eternal life; and I will raise him up at the last day" (John 6:54). Jesus did not say, "He that cometh and drinketh of My soul and of My mind and of My spirit," but, "He that eateth My flesh." The flesh is body. If we dedicate

our bodies to God, we might win this world for Him. When people see that we have taken our own flesh and blood and dedicated them to God, they see something they have never seen before. What a precious promise of eternal life from God—the resurrection from the dead through understanding the Holy Communion.

> *And he said unto them, This is my blood of the new testament, which is shed for many.* (Mark 14:24)

"Likewise also the cup after supper, saying, This cup is the new testament in my blood, which is shed for you" (Luke 22:20). You may say, "He said it many times." That is what I want you to realize. We are building on the context of the whole of the Word of God. God sent a body from heaven. His name is Jesus. That body is our example on the face of this earth. He gave that body as a sacrifice. We see here that the blood of the Lord Jesus Christ is your redemption factor.

"Whom God hath set forth to be a propitiation through faith in his blood, to declare his righteousness for the remission of sins that are past, through the forbearance of God" (Romans 3:25). It was the blood that flowed through His veins.

We often speak of the emotions of Jesus. We speak of His great faith. We desire His love and identify with His body. Humans can identify with the body of Jesus. Jesus gave His body to save the human soul.

Man's Identification in Heaven

Heaven understands us through Jesus. Christ is our Advocate at this moment. When we say that we are hurting, He says, "Father, I had a body down there.

That is how I used to hurt, too. Now You take that hurt away." The Father replies, "Yes, I will do it." That body in heaven is an identification for you. The purpose of Jesus' earthly body was to represent the redeemed in heaven.

In His earthly body, Christ is known as the Last Adam. First Corinthians 15:45–47 says,

> *And so it is written, The first man Adam was made a living soul; the last Adam was made a quickening spirit. Howbeit that was not first which is spiritual, but that which is natural; and afterward that which is spiritual. The first man is of the earth, earthy: the second man is the Lord from heaven.*

Man was given a second chance to please God. He fell on his face and missed the whole purpose of being in the Garden of Eden. God sent a Second Adam, His Son, and clothed Him in a human body so He could be the Second Adam. He defeated and destroyed the devil to bring you into a right relationship with the Father God. The Bible teaches that this was man's second and last chance when Christ came as the Second Adam.

"Neither by the blood of goats and calves, but by his own blood he entered in once into the holy place, having obtained eternal redemption for us" (Hebrews 9:12). The blood of bulls and goats was not enough. His own body's blood was taken into the holy place. There it obtained eternal redemption. His own blood obtained eternal redemption for humankind.

> *Having therefore, brethren, boldness to enter into the holiest by the blood of Jesus, by a new and living way, which he hath consecrated for us, through the veil, that is to say, his flesh.* (Hebrews 10:19–20)

God was able to move into our inner parts through the veil of human flesh. He could correct, heal, or convert; whatever was needed. The Lord Jesus Christ is our hope.

> *Wherefore Jesus also, that he might sanctify the people with his own blood, suffered without the gate.*
> (Hebrews 13:12).

The flesh of the Lord Jesus Christ is our altar where His sacrifice was offered up before God and accepted. That is an eternal and universal restitution.

We Are God's Treasure

> *And they sung a new song, saying, Thou art worthy to take the book, and to open the seals thereof: for thou wast slain, and hast redeemed us to God by thy blood out of every kindred, and tongue, and people, and nation.* (Revelation 5:9)

Christ is a universal Savior! All races and peoples are redeemed by His blood.

Second Corinthians 4:7 says that we have this treasure *"in earthen vessels."* This treasure in earthen vessels is our bodies, *"that the excellency of the power may be of God, and not of us."* We carry this excellent treasure, the treasure of heaven, in an earthen vessel. You are the earthen vessel. That is the reason why you should be careful about your body. You carry heaven's treasure in that body. When you wake up in the morning and look in the mirror, look at the body and say, "This is an earthen vessel that carries the excellency of the power of God." You will smile when you see it. This creates a whole new world.

Second Corinthians 4:10 says, *"Always bearing about in the body the dying of the Lord Jesus."* Paul did not say that we were carrying about Jesus' emotions or His will. He did not even say that we were carrying His spirit. The word says, *"Always bearing about in the body the dying of the Lord Jesus, that the life also of Jesus might be made manifest in our body."* We would get a quickness in our step if we studied this properly and saw that we are more than we thought we were. We are the tabernacles of divinity walking on the face of this earth. We carry the image of divine redemption in our bodies.

"For we which live are alway delivered unto death for Jesus' sake, that the life also of Jesus might be made manifest in our mortal flesh" (2 Corinthians 4:11). We try to get Jesus into our spirits and soulical emotions, so that we might manifest Christ; but the Word says our mortal flesh is supposed to manifest Christ. This includes our mouth, ears, eyes, tongue, hands, and feet.

The reason many Christians are sick is that their bodies are not in Jesus Christ like they ought to be. We should examine ourselves and see if our dedication to Jesus is like it should be.

> For God, who commanded the light to shine out of darkness, hath shined in our hearts, to give the light of the knowledge of the glory of God in the face of Jesus Christ. (2 Corinthians 4:6)

Jesus' Submission at Calvary

At Calvary, it was Jesus' body, soul, and spirit in mighty divine unity that saved this world. It was the total man of the total spirit, soul, and body!

Man's body can be rebellious, but Jesus' body was not rebellious. When Christ cried in the garden, *"Not my will, but thine, be done"* (Luke 22:42), it was His body. It was His body that would be lashed with a Roman whip and nailed to the cross. They could not nail His mind or His spirit to the cross.

The flesh of Jesus did not draw back. Our flesh must not draw back. The body of Christ did not refuse to share in the redemption of the human race. The body marched to the cross to bear its share. The soldiers cut His back with deep stripes from the Roman whip. They plucked His beard from His face by the handfuls. It was twisted and pulled in madness. Long sharp thorns were made into a mock crown to cut deep into His fore-head, causing His human blood to run down His face. It happened to His body.

The Roman nails, forged in a blacksmith's shop of the Roman Empire, pierced those sacred feet with inde-scribable pain. The double-edged sword of the battles of the Roman Empire plunged into His human side to quicken His death.

By His blood we are saved and healed. Christ died physically. Christ died humanly, to save the human race.

What Does Jesus Look Like?

The Bible does not declare the features of the body of Jesus. Nowhere in the Bible can you find what Jesus' human face looked like. None of the Gospels reveal it. Nowhere do you read of the height of His human body—whether short, tall, or medium. You do not find it in the Bible. Portraits of Jesus are the opinion of the artist.

Why? Very simple. He does not want men wor-shipping His natural body. He wants us worshipping God. No one knows the color of Jesus' eyes. You may say, "But we will see Him in heaven." Yes, and Revelation says His eyes are like burning coals and flaming suns. No one knows the size of His feet or the length of His hair.

Jesus said in John 4:23, *"But the hour cometh, and now is, when the true worshippers shall worship the Father in spirit and in truth: for the Father seeketh such to worship him."* So let us worship the Most High God!

10

The Redeemed and Everlasting Body

◆◆◆

Man groans for the final expression of immortality, the final fulfillment of the hope of the human body.

And not only they, but ourselves also, which have the firstfruits of the Spirit, even we ourselves groan within ourselves, waiting for the adoption, to wit, the redemption of our body. For we are saved by hope: but hope that is seen is not hope: for what a man seeth, why doth he yet hope for? But if we hope for that we see not, then do we with patience wait for it. Likewise the Spirit also helpeth our infirmities: for we know not what we should pray for as we ought: but the Spirit itself maketh intercession for us with groanings which cannot be uttered.
(Romans 8:23–26)

This is an amazing portrayal of the true human hope. It is not a hallucinating human body on drugs or alcohol, but the real human person in divine expectancy.

For we that are in this tabernacle do groan, being burdened: not for that we would be unclothed, but clothed upon, that mortality might be swallowed up of life.
(2 Corinthians 5:4)

The Body Looks for Transformation

Human frailty is very evident in the bodies of people. The human body looks for transformation.

*And though after my skin worms destroy this body,
yet in my flesh shall I see God.* (Job 19:26)

The book of Job is said to be earth's oldest piece of literature. It is amazing to read such an ancient account of a redeemed and everlasting body.

*But some man will say, How are the dead raised up?
and with what body do they come? Thou fool, that
which thou sowest is not quickened, except it die: and
that which thou sowest, thou sowest not that body
that shall be, but bare grain, it may chance of wheat,
or of some other grain: but God giveth it a body as
it hath pleased him, and to every seed his own body.
All flesh is not the same flesh: but there is one kind of
flesh of men, another flesh of beasts, another of fishes,
and another of birds. There are also celestial bodies,
and bodies terrestrial: but the glory of the celestial is
one, and the glory of the terrestrial is another. There
is one glory of the sun, and another glory of the moon,
and another glory of the stars: for one star differeth
from another star in glory. So also is the resurrection
of the dead. It is sown in corruption; it is raised in
incorruption: it is sown in dishonour; it is raised in
glory: it is sown in weakness; it is raised in power: it
is sown a natural body; it is raised a spiritual body.
There is a natural body, and there is a spiritual body.*
(1 Corinthians 15:35–44)

What a statement! What excitement! This truth removes the fear of the future. It puts a golden frame around physical death, knowing it is only a cosmic transition.

Jesus—First Begotten of the Dead

The everlastingness of a man's existence is observed in how that man's body bears the hallmark of eternalness.

> *And from Jesus Christ, who is the faithful witness, and the first begotten of the dead, and the prince of the kings of the earth. Unto him that loved us, and washed us from our sins in his own blood.* (Revelation 1:5)

Because we are in Christ, of Christ, and represent Christ, we accept Him as the first begotten of the dead. As He lives so we will live.

It was God the Father who promised an everlasting, immortal body. *"For God so loved the world, that he gave his only begotten Son, that whosoever believeth in him should not perish, but have everlasting life"* (John 3:16). What greater proof could man desire?

Christ, in John 4:10, said, *"If thou knewest the gift of God, and who it is that saith to thee, Give me to drink; thou wouldest have asked of him, and he would have given thee living water."*

It is further stated in John 4:13–14,

> *Jesus answered and said unto her, Whosoever drinketh of this water shall thirst again: but whosoever drinketh of the water that I shall give him shall never thirst; but the water that I shall give him shall be in him a well of water springing up into everlasting life.*

The witness of two will establish every word. John 6:39–40 says,

> *And this is the Father's will which hath sent me, that of all which he hath given me I should lose nothing, but should raise it up again at the last day. And this is the will of him that sent me, that every one which seeth the Son, and believeth on him, may have everlasting life: and I will raise him up at the last day.*

A person who disbelieves man's immortality destroys the very heart of God's Word. John 11:25–26 says,

> *Jesus said unto her, I am the resurrection, and the life: he that believeth in me, though he were dead, yet shall he live: and whosoever liveth and believeth in me shall never die. Believest thou this?*

He is still asking you and me, *"Believest thou this?"*

> *Let not your heart be troubled: ye believe in God, believe also in me. In my Father's house are many mansions: if it were not so, I would have told you. I go to prepare a place for you. And if I go and prepare a place for you, I will come again, and receive you unto myself; that where I am, there ye may be also.* (John 14:1–3)

> *These words spake Jesus, and lifted up his eyes to heaven, and said, Father, the hour is come; glorify thy Son, that thy Son also may glorify thee: as thou hast given him power over all flesh, that he should give eternal life to as many as thou hast given him. And this is life eternal, that they might know thee the only true God, and Jesus Christ, whom thou hast sent.* (John 17:1–3)

> *Blessed be the God and Father of our Lord Jesus Christ, which according to his abundant mercy hath begotten us again unto a lively hope by the resurrection of Jesus*

Christ from the dead, to an inheritance incorruptible, and undefiled, and that fadeth not away, reserved in heaven for you. (1 Peter 1:3–4)

Paul sought the new body when he said in 2 Corinthians 5:8, *"We are confident, I say, and willing rather to be absent from the body, and to be present with the Lord."*

Henceforth there is laid up for me a crown of righteousness, which the Lord, the righteous judge, shall give me at that day: and not to me only, but unto all them also that love his appearing. (2 Timothy 4:8)

The eternal uniting of the immortals is stated in 1 Corinthians 15:50–58,

Now this I say, brethren, that flesh and blood cannot inherit the kingdom of God; neither doth corruption inherit incorruption. Behold, I show you a mystery; we shall not all sleep, but we shall all be changed, in a moment, in the twinkling of an eye, at the last trump: for the trumpet shall sound, and the dead shall be raised incorruptible, and we shall be changed. For this corruptible must put on incorruption, and this mortal must put on immortality. So when this corruptible shall have put on incorruption, and this mortal shall have put on immortality, then shall be brought to pass the saying that is written, Death is swallowed up in victory. O death, where is thy sting? O grave, where is thy victory? The sting of death is sin; and the strength of sin is the law. But thanks be to God, which giveth us the victory through our Lord Jesus Christ. Therefore, my beloved brethren, be ye stedfast, unmoveable, always abounding in the work of the Lord, forasmuch as ye know that your labour is not in vain in the Lord.

11

Your Soul—The Adamic Nature

The human soul is the old creation of Adam. From the Greek word for soul, *psuche,* we derive words like *psychology, psychiatry,* and *psychoanalysis.* They do not come from the born-again, supernatural nature God puts within us.

First Corinthians 2:14 says, *"But the natural man receiveth not the things of the Spirit of God: for they are foolishness unto him."* It is hard to accept that, but it is true. You have a conflict within you. Your soulical parts want to dominate your spiritual parts. Paul told us in Romans that we have to fight until we subdue it. If you are not careful, your Adamic nature will laugh at your born-again nature. You can accumulate all the facts and information needed for a Ph.D., but you will not know God through that degree. You will know God by saying, "Bring that spiritual, born-again nature into me and revive the spirit part of me!" Immediately new things begin to come into your mind; new feelings begin to come into your emotions, and you become a new person in the Lord Jesus Christ.

The Battle for Authority

Your soulical parts have at least three dominant areas or "worlds." The first world of your soul is the

mind, your thought center. No person has ever pene-
trated the depths of the abilities that God has instilled
within the human mind.

The second tremendous element within the soul is
your emotional life. Now these worlds are like chains.

Sometimes you cannot tell where emotion ends
and thought begins, or where thought ends and emotions begin. They are intricately integrated within our
inner being. Each person is a world of emotions. If you
want to have some fun, get a long piece of paper and
begin in the morning to write down every emotion you
have all day long. You will be simply amazed by the
emotions exhibited in only one day. You are an emotional creature. Emotion is beautiful when it is tied
to your born-again nature. If your spirit is not born
again, anger rises up within you like a lion; fear rises
up within you to destroy you; hate rises up within you
until your emotional world becomes dangerous. Unregenerate emotion can destroy you. It can destroy your
family. It can destroy your business. You can come into
your job with a sour face for a few days and your work
will be finished. If you own the business, it will be finished, and you will be broke. You cannot bring a bad
spirit and emotion into your business.

The third world of the soul is the area of decision,
your willpower. Your will is a very remarkable thing.
Again, the soulical areas are so interlinked, it is difficult to tell where the mind and will finish or begin.
In the will area of the soul, without God, a person can
become stubborn and very difficult for anybody to get
along with. Even the Lord Jesus said, *"Not my will, but
thine, be done"* (Luke 22:42). He had to submit the will of
His Adamic nature to the Father. He said, "I don't want
My will." Your will can drive you to all kinds of bad
situations, bad business, bad marriages, and so on.

Now these are the three basic areas of your second man—your soul. This is the real you that you were born with. These soulical areas are never right until they are born again by the Spirit of God. We never feel right until we have Jesus in our hearts. Our emotions are never correct until we know God.

Learn to Speak to Yourself

Smith Wigglesworth told me, "I don't ever ask Smith Wigglesworth how he feels." I said, "Sir, you are Smith Wigglesworth." He said, "But Smith Wigglesworth never asks Smith Wigglesworth how he feels." What in the world did he mean? He was saying the same thing that David said. "Why art thou cast down, O my soul? Rejoice thou in the Lord." (See Psalm 42:5.) David was talking to David. The spirit-man of David was talking to the soulical man of David, saying, "David, get up out of that gutter. Stop being sad, and start rejoicing in the Lord. Get busy; rejoice in Jehovah!"

In many churches as much as a third of the whole congregation is depressed and sad. They are people not living in the spirit; they are living in the soulical realm. Depression and sadness are not from heaven. God's kingdom, which is in you, is God's righteousness, peace, and joy. It has nothing to do with sadness and depression. If you live in your soulical and emotional parts, you are not living in your spiritual parts. Your spiritual part must command your mind.

Exercising your own will by making deliberate decisions of choice without God is living in the Adamic, soulical parts in the volitional area.

The Soul—"The Carnal Man"

The soul of man is actually the center and core of the human personality. It is the natural part. We call it the carnal part. It reveals man in what we can know of him—whether he has a sharp mind or not, what kind of decisions he makes, whether others can tolerate him or not—and his willpower.

The soul of man is seductive, deceptive, seeking its own self-interest, and craving for carnal gratification. If you do not master it, it will never be subject to the Most High God. Some might ask, "Can't God do that?" No, God comes into your life and puts a spirit within you. The spirit within you deals with the other parts of your being. You are responsible for it. God desires that only the spirit of man will decide that man's destiny. What we call our human nature is the function of our soulical being. This is what you have to struggle against in your spiritual life to be an overcomer.

Sometimes your soulical parts seem very nice. You can be naturally a very gentle person, but the moment you are not pleased, you will refuse to be gentle anymore. A man may walk into a house as gentle as you can imagine. He looks inside and sees his wife kiss another man. Then he suddenly loses all his gentleness and becomes a raging lion. The veneer of your soulical parts in our civilization is just a thin covering. God is love, and the attribute of God is love. Man, in all his activities, will say, "I'm going to reach out and be spiritual." But he cannot succeed unless he is born again. Man is naturally gentle unless he wants to be otherwise. When he gets irritated, then he refuses to be gentle.

When it's in trial, the force of human nature will react opposite to what you think your soulish nature is like. When you are suffering, when something goes against you, or when you are not pleased, your soul becomes something else. That is when people say, "Oh, that's not like me."

Submit Yourself to God

The power and the abilities of the soul of man must not be destroyed. Jesus said, "I did not come to destroy; I came to fulfill." He does not want to destroy the keen mind, magnificent emotions, or strong will. He did not come to destroy them; He came to use them for the kingdom of God.

If Hitler had become an evangelist and used all the potential of his soul, he would have become the greatest evangelist who ever lived. He had the qualities there, but he would not allow Jesus to tame them. Millions of people are like that today. When God, through the human spirit that He has placed within man, is allowed to rule human life, man can have a beautiful and successful life.

12
The Works of the Soul

Man's soulish forces have been active throughout the millennia. For example, man's soulical being created and made the Tower of Babel after the Flood. This Tower of Babel that man conceived in his own mind was to be his deliverance. He was trying to tell God, "Send another flood if You want to; we'll climb our tower. You'll never be able to get us." Man has always, with his mind, wanted to seek that which God did not want him to seek. The result of the Tower of Babel was about three thousand different languages in the world, creating chaos, confusion, and conflict. Tongues have always been a barrier. When you meet a person with whom you cannot communicate, there is a barrier. Even if he speaks your own language but lisps when he speaks, or does not pronounce words according to your area, a barrier of friendship and many other problems may arise.

On the other hand, man's spirit, not his soul, built Noah's ark. It was another building project. One was created out of man's soul and caused chaos. The other was created out of man's spirit and brought deliverance to the world. God is not against building. He is against building in the soulical parts, which has to do with your mind without God. On the other hand, the building of the spiritual parts has to do with doing things from God's point of view rather than the devil's point of view.

A very good example of this chemistry of the soul has to do with Israel's first king.

King Saul began living and walking according to his spirit. First Samuel 10:6 says, *"And the spirit of the LORD will come upon thee, and thou shalt prophesy with them, and shalt be turned into another man."* Saul was to receive a new heart. This meant he began in the spirit. He was to prophesy, which is of the spirit.

> *And let it be, when these signs are come unto thee, that thou do as occasion serve thee; for God is with thee. And thou shalt go down before me to Gilgal; and, behold, I will come down unto thee, to offer burnt offerings, and to sacrifice sacrifices of peace offerings: seven days shalt thou tarry, till I come to thee, and show thee what thou shalt do. And it was so, that when he had turned his back to go from Samuel, God gave him another heart: and all those signs came to pass that day.* (vv. 7–9)

Saul was a man who began in the spirit. He began moving by the power of God. Any time a person begins right, the devil does not want him to stay right. The devil wants you to go off into a humanistic manner of living. He wants you to go back into Adamic principles of rebellion.

> *And Samuel said to Saul, Thou hast done foolishly: thou hast not kept the commandment of the LORD thy God, which he commanded thee: for now would the LORD have established thy kingdom upon Israel for ever.* (1 Samuel 13:13)

When you live dominated by your soulical parts, the Bible says you are living foolishly. The Adamic nature is the spirit of rebellion. It is the separator from the living God, from peace in our hearts and joy in our lives.

If you live in your soulical being, your kingdom will not continue. God was seeking a man after His own heart. God went looking for another man. The Lord had commanded Saul to be the captain over His people. His eyes (his body) saw the wealth—the gold, silver, the beautiful raiment—and he wanted it. His soulical pride saw King Agag and he said, "I'll bring him back as a trophy." When Samuel met him, Samuel called it rebellion. In 1 Samuel 15:23 he said, *"For rebellion is as the sin of witchcraft, and stubbornness is as iniquity and idolatry. Because thou hast rejected the word of the LORD, he hath also rejected thee from being king."* Some people are willing to give God a gift, but they are not really interested in Him. They stay away from church or go somewhere they should not go. They think that giving God a gift will calm Him down.

The Results of Rebellion

After Saul revolted against God, notice what happened to him.

(1) According to the Bible, he became depressed. He became so sad that his servants hired people to play musical instruments and sing in his presence, hoping to take the sadness away from him. Depression is not from God. It is a soulical condition that belongs to the human mind and has no relationship with God, God's blessing, or God's power. When you are depressed, do not blame it on God. God does not depress. Sin and the soulical nature in rebellion against God depress people. Find out where your depression comes from, and you will discover that it has no relationship with

the divine precepts of God. It has no relationship with loving and serving God.

(2) Hate against his successor came into his heart. He believed David would take the throne away from him and began to hate the young man. Hatred is a thing of the soul. Hate is love gone sour. It moves from the spirit of man into the soul of man. You show hate with the same instrument that you use to express love. The spirit within you that should cause you to love moves over into another area called antipathy, and you begin to hate. The Bible says hate gives birth to murder.

Saul first took his javelin and tried to kill David. Then he took his sword, went after him in the field, and said, "I will kill you." I think it is very interesting to see how the soulical parts work without God. First comes depression, then hate, murder, and finally witchcraft. When he could not get anything from God, he went to the witch, and said, "Say, Gal, do you have anything from God for me? What is God going to do to me? Am I going to die or live?" That is how the soulical parts of a person can lead a person totally outside the will of God.

We have seen that the human mind is a department of the human soul. It is one of the most important parts of the human personality. Romans 1:28 says, *"And even as they did not like to retain God in their knowledge, God gave them over to a reprobate mind, to do those things which are not convenient."* Man without God, without the Bible, and without the Spirit has a reprobate mind inside him. It is a part of your soul. A reprobate mind is a mind in absolute anger and set against God. It has gone away from God and into the dirt of sin and confusion. It has to be changed by God's supernatural power to be anything else other than reprobate.

When a man will not be spiritual, he becomes carnal. There is no middle ground. Either you have a mind subject to the Spirit and laws of God or you have a reprobate mind. We have to decide if we are going to function in our humanistic mind or in our divinely engrafted spirit. However, all too many Christians live in their reprobate minds. God has given them the new birth; yet rather than living in the Spirit, they have moved into rebellion by saying, "I do not want to retain God in my knowledge whatsoever."

Romans 8:7 says, *"Because the carnal mind is enmity against God: for it is not subject to the law of God, neither indeed can be."* You are born with the Adamic mind. That is the reason you have the rebirth of the spirit.

It is not easy to study our inward parts. They are beyond our human vision and hearing. On the inside of us is the inner man. This is the part we must really dissect and study. We must say, "Where do all my actions and feelings come from?" They come from one of two sources—either from the non-born-again nature of your Adamic carnal being, or from the born-again nature where God puts into you His righteousness, His peace, and His joy. You are the decision-maker. You will have to decide whether they come up out of your spirit or your soul. If they come up out of your soul, the Bible says they are carnal and not subject to the law of God.

The Mind in Warfare against God

Because of Adam, your natural mind has a hatred toward God. It is in warfare against God. It is not subject to the law of God, neither indeed can it be. No sinner can ever live in great peace with God. No unregenerate person can ever live in the glow of the spirit. That is not possible. You can live in the spirit only by being born of the spirit. You can walk with God only when your feet are shod with the preparation of the Gospel of the Lord Jesus Christ. The beginning of the new man is a born-again experience. From there your spirit begins to dominate your life, the power of God comes into you, and your mind becomes a servant rather than a king.

In Ephesians 4:17, the great apostle Paul said these words, *"This I say therefore, and testify in the Lord, that ye henceforth walk not as other Gentiles walk, in the vanity of their mind."* The unregenerate person walks in the vanity of his mind. You have only to study human beings a very short time to see how tremendously real that verse is. The mind without Jesus, the Bible, prayer, and the moving of the power of the Holy Spirit is full of emptiness, human vanity, and that which comes and goes. There is nothing permanent or solid about it. God wants you and me to live by our spirits and by the Holy Spirit within us. He does not want us to live in the vanity of the unregenerate human mind.

The Word of God says further in Colossians 2:18, *"Let no man beguile you of your reward in a voluntary humility and worshipping of angels, intruding into those things which he hath not seen, vainly puffed up by his fleshly mind."* Pride comes out of the old Adamic nature. Often we see a person with seemingly great humility telling others to worship angels, denominations, or doctrines. He is actually puffed up in his fleshly mind and is not spiritual. This is the origin of problems in churches. They come through the vanity of the inflated fleshly mind that has nothing to do with God. They are of the human nature and the devil. They have no relationship to spiritual things.

Psalm 94:11 says, *"The LORD knoweth the thoughts of man, that they are vanity."* We might hide our thoughts from others, but not from Jehovah. God knows the thoughts of the unregenerate person. When He comes into you, He gives you a spirit. That spirit begins to cover your mind and says, "Mind, think the ways of God. Think the ways of purity. Think the ways of holiness, and I will fill you with good things, such as the Word of God, prayer, praise, and fellowship. I will fill you with good things that will cause you not to have the vanity of being puffed up within your own mind."

What Is the Heart of Man?

The heart is an organ. It is a part of the soul, like other organs of the body. Death comes if it does not function. Proverbs 23:7 says, *"As he thinketh in his heart, so is he."* As a man thinks all the time in his heart, as he dominates and promotes his emotions, that is what that man is.

In Jeremiah 4:14, God says, *"O Jerusalem, wash thine heart from wickedness, that thou mayest be saved. How long shall thy vain thoughts lodge within thee?"* God put the heart and emotions together. They are two soulical elements bound together like a chain. God put the two of them together so that your emotions and heart function in unison. Your heart says it and your emotions do it. That is one of the other areas of your soulical being. Matthew 9:4 says, *"And Jesus knowing their thoughts said, Wherefore think ye evil in your hearts?"* The human heart and the human emotions flow together. The heart says to the emotions, "Look angry; let your eyes look angry. Let your face look angry. Let your words sound angry." Jesus said, "Why do you think evil in your hearts?"

He also said in Matthew 15:19, *"For out of the heart proceed evil thoughts, murders, adulteries, fornications, thefts, false witness, blasphemies."* These things come up out of the great vast dimension of the emotional part of the human being that is part of his Adamic nature. If this soulical nature is not controlled and dominated by the spirit, it will lead him the wrong way every time.

"And God saw that the wickedness of man was great in the earth, and that every imagination of the thoughts of his heart was only evil continually" (Genesis 6:5). God had to judge this wickedness with the Flood.

13
The Chemistry of the Soul

◆●◆

*T*he Word of God says in 1 Corinthians 2:13, *"Which things also we speak, not in the words which man's wisdom teacheth, but which the Holy Ghost teacheth; comparing spiritual things with spiritual."* The soul has to do with the earth, with man's fallen nature. Men fall into lies very easily. Science and philosophy change all the time. At one time man thought the world was flat, yet God had spoken about the circle of the earth a thousand years before Jesus was born. Soulical men listen to man's wisdom, but not to what the Holy Spirit teaches comparing things with the spiritual world.

Verse 14 says, *"But the natural man receiveth not the things of the Spirit of God: for they are foolishness unto him: neither can he know them, because they are spiritually discerned."* A sinner cannot understand why you go to church. The Bible says it is foolishness to him because his spirit is dormant. He has no enlightenment in his spirit. He finds it impossible to understand anything about spiritual things.

What happens to the heart and emotions of man when he gives himself to God? If you live by your feelings you are always going to be out of communication with God. However, we can have authority over our feelings. David, a thousand years before Jesus was born, spoke to his own soul and said, "Soul, rejoice." His spirit talked to his soul. David's own human spirit was talking to his emotions saying, "Emotions, feel good." Smith Wigglesworth told me, "I get up every morning and I praise and magnify God. I even dance before Jesus. My emotions are servants to my spirit, and that is what my spirit wants." The Word of God teaches us in Ezekiel 18:31, *"Cast away from you all your transgressions, whereby ye have transgressed; and make you a new heart and a new spirit."*

God gives you new emotions when He gives you a new spirit. When the heart is under the direction of the spirit, it is a holy, joyful, peaceful thing that God wants within the human personality. David's spirit controlled his emotions. Psalm 84:2 says, *"My soul longeth, yea, even fainteth for the courts of the LORD: my heart and my flesh crieth out for the living God."* I do not believe that there are many people like that today. David said so many revealing and enlightening things about worship. *"I was glad when they said unto me, Let us go into the house of the LORD"* (Psalm 122:1). When the servant knocked on the door and said, "Oh, King, time for church," David must have begun to dance and say, "Praise God! Hallelujah Jehovah! I'm ready! I'm ready! Let's go to the house of the Lord." He did not drag his feet with reluctance like some of us do.

His spirit dominated his soulical parts, which have to do with his emotional area. David made his soulical part subservient to his spiritual part. If we do not do the same, we cannot be what God wants us to be. We cannot be the light of the world until we become commanders of our soulical parts.

Your Emotions Must Be under the Direction of Your Spirit

Job 23:16 says, *"For God maketh my heart soft, and the Almighty troubleth me."* He made his emotions soft before Him. If your emotions get hard, mean, and calloused, you cannot be what God wants you to be. Your spirit is born of God. The born-again nature that you received on the day you were saved must be the dominating factor in your life to make your emotions obey. If you permit your emotions to be king, they will drive you to the end of the earth like a wild storm on the sea. Your emotions are uncontrollable without the spirit and the power of God.

"And the multitude of them that believed were of one heart and of one soul: neither said any of them that ought of the things which he possessed was his own; but they had all things common" (Acts 4:32). Emotionally, you want to grab this and grab that. You want to have this and have that. Emotion desires this and desires that, but when the church was at its best, the members were one emotionally. Everyone exalted and praised God for His wonderful blessings and mighty power. They flowed together in the Spirit. The church in Jerusalem possibly had several hundred thousand members in it. They were the people who had one heart and one emotion before the Lord.

"Servants, obey in all things your masters according to the flesh; not with eyeservice, as menpleasers; but in singleness of heart, fearing God" (Colossians 3:22). If you are going to serve, have the right spirit about it. There are a lot of people who work in a factory all day long, and it is drudgery. If you live by your spirit, you can be just as happy with a screwdriver as you are with a songbook or plowing a field as you are sitting in the pew—if you want to be!

If you let the devil say "This is hard; I can't do it!" the first thing you know your whole being is going to be out of tune with God because you permitted your emotions to have their wild, Adamic actions. We need to have spirit-dominated actions by giving our emotions to God and flowing with God in our emotional beings. He says, "Not with eyeservice, as menpleasers, but in singleness of your inner being." This means that our emotions are under the divine prerogatives of God. Then it says, *"fearing God,"* which comes only when we have the proper respect for God and know God is God, and we are just men.

"And the peace of God, which passeth all understanding, shall keep your hearts and minds through Christ Jesus" (Philippians 4:7). God's emotion of peace surpasses all human intellectualism. This peace will keep your heart and emotions. It will also keep your mind and thoughts. Joy in your emotions can flow into your mind, purify it, wash it clean, and make it sweet and blessed inside you.

The Life Is in the Blood

What is the human blood that flows through your veins? It is like a river that begins in the mountains and comes down to wash away all the mess, muck, and filthy humanity. The river carries them out to sea, where God purifies the water with salt and many other elements. He purifies it again by vaporizing it, taking it up into the clouds, and dropping it again on the mountaintops. Then it runs down again. Rivers are God's cleansing system for the face of the earth, and your blood is the cleansing system for the body. The blood that flows through you is a cleansing power.

The blood is the life flow of the soul and the body of man. Leviticus 17:11 says, *"For the life of the flesh is in the blood."* Your life is not in your bones or muscles. Your life is in your blood. God has given it upon the altar for an atonement for your soul. This is done in order for your old nature to be changed and your old life to be renewed. When Jesus came, He had to give His blood because the blood makes an atonement for the soul. Nothing else can make atonement. That is the reason the heathen still use blood. Witchcraft uses the blood of chickens and small animals. They use blood because the devil always counterfeits God. The devil has never been known to do anything original. God has declared that your life is in your blood. It is your bloodstream that purifies your brain. Your brain must have a flow of blood or it will die. The blood flows throughout your body, purifying, rejuvenating, bringing strength, and producing power.

The heart, the seat of your emotions, is the pump that sends that life throughout your whole being. That could mean that if you are wrong in your emotions, you are wrong everywhere. If you do not have your emotions under control, your whole person will be affected. The emotions of the heart are what project the blood of life. Good emotions project life that makes you a new person, a new thing, and a new power.

We are not seeing the heart as the doctor sees it, of course. We see it as the contributing factor to your soulical personality.

14
The Human Will

———————◆●◆———————

*T*he human will is vast. Jesus was the master of His will when He said, *"Not my will, but thine, be done"* (Luke 22:42). This is the supreme example of the spirit being alive in power and authority. If the will is in rebellion, you are in trouble. Your soulical parts (your mind, emotions, and will) are important. We must look down inside them to see what they are and know when they function in God and when they function in the Adamic nature.

The will is a *major force* in the universe. If you have a Strong's Concordance, you will notice that the words *will, willfully,* and *willingly* take up about twelve pages of the concordance. I discovered each page had about three hundred and sixty references, which is more than four thousand references to *will*. It looks like God is trying to get our attention when He puts four thousand references on any subject in the Bible.

I have spent considerable time in seeking God and thinking about the *will*. I trust you will join me with your heart open and with your spirit open so that we may discover things about yourself and about God.

Who Has Will

There are at least six distinct creatures in our universe who possess will, or willpower. Willpower is a dominant factor regarding destiny for rational persons. You are what you are by will. You spend eternity in heaven or hell by your will.

The human will is one-third of the human soulical personality. God wants us to understand the force of willpower, to identify it as it functions. He wants us to know by divine decree that you and I can be victorious in every department of our created being.

We will observe that God, the Creator of all things, possesses willpower. He is the Originator of willpower. When we find out what willpower is in God, we can see what willpower is to you.

We will observe that Jesus Christ, God's only begotten Son, possessed tremendous willpower. He functioned in willpower. If we understand this we can say, "The willpower that was in the Lord Jesus Christ can function in my life." You will be able to coordinate the truth of willpower by observing it first in God the Father, and then in God the Son.

We also seek to penetrate the third entity of the Holy Trinity, the Holy Spirit, and learn that He exerts amazing, mighty willpower.

Angels obey God by option. They do not have to obey God; they will to obey God. They are not slaves; they are not without opinion, and they are not without decision. Every time God speaks they exert willpower to obey or disobey.

On the negative side, all demons possess willpower, and the devil has strong willpower. Demons use their willpower to combat the purpose of God in the universe.

When you observe willpower in such a panoramic view from God the Father, to Satan, and all between, you may say, "Why didn't I know that before?" You cannot live a victorious Christian life without having some recognition that deep down inside you are the forces that really control you. Those forces, if they are directed by God, can lead you in the right direction. Those forces, dominated by the devil, will put you on the wrong road.

God Created the Will of Man

Man, the Homo sapiens species that God created and placed on planet Earth, is the apex of God's creation. Man was endowed with sovereign willpower. This endowment of power was granted to man by divine prerogative. God said, "I will create this person and call him 'man.' I will give him willpower." In doing so, God made him a creature of judgment. He made him a creature of understanding. He made him a creature of decision. You do not have to go straight ahead; you can go backward if you want. You do not have to turn to the right; you can go to the left if you want. God places in you the amazing volitional strengths, anointings, and powers of what we call *will*.

When God granted you this will, He determined to never violate it. Sometimes you say, "Why didn't God stop Hitler? Why didn't God stop this, that, or the other?" God has granted us decision power. He has granted us willpower, and God will not violate it. He will let you eventually be lost if you want to be. God will not violate man's willpower.

The devil cannot violate it. I have talked to some of the most extreme cases of devil possession on the face of the earth. Every one of them told me that they did not have to obey the devil.

With sufficient willpower determined against your mind, most persons can be hypnotized. It is the giving over of the will that permits you to be hypnotized.

If a person resists the hypnotist with his will, a message is sent up to the mind or brain, saying, "I resist this person seeking to take over my mind and hypnotize me." That person cannot be hypnotized. The mind obeys the will. That is where we seek to determine the greatness of the will, when it supersedes the mind. The will must first be broken down before the other parts of your being will cooperate with hypnotism and say, "Yes, we will go along with that."

The will cannot be weighed on a scale. You cannot measure the will. The will is different from your corporeal person, such as your eyes, your hands, or your feet. These can be seen and felt, but your will goes beyond that part of your total personality. It is a strong thing that governs. It governs your hands, feet, seeing, hearing, and so forth. Man is blessed by his Creator to possess a threefold personality. The will is a third part of your soulical being. Your soulical being is your mind, your emotions, and your will. The will can be destroyed, polluted, and broken down with alcohol or drugs. Then a human person cannot exercise will as God created it to function. The will is to be a protected part of your personality.

When man is using or operating in his soulical parts, he is using his mind, emotions, or will. He can be using two or even three parts of his soul at the same time. For example, his mind and his will can be functioning simultaneously. He wills to do something, the idea is conveyed to the mind, and the mind carries it out. It can be something of a fantastic nature and the emotions would jump in and say, "I'm glad. I'm glad." Then he would have all three of his soulical portions functioning at one time. When man is not functioning by his mind or his emotions, he is operating in the area of his will. He wills to do a certain thing. So his will is in action at that point, determining what he will be in all the parts of his total personality.

The will can be moved and activated by three elements.

1) Divine spiritual power
2) Human power
3) Demonic power

This means the will of man can be motivated by God, man himself, or satanic forces.

To analyze the will we must observe that it is a power manifested by intelligence; whether it is deity, angels, mankind, or devils. *Without intelligence there is no will.*

Wish

To will is to wish. It is related to willingness, or an assent to perform. If you do not will to do a thing, you become unwilling. That means that your will goes into reverse. For example, God said to me, "Will you go to Manila, Philippines, and be a missionary?" I said, "I will." I didn't say, "I think or feel." I said, "I will." So God's will and my will got together, and I took my family to the Philippines. My reward was that God gave us the greatest revival we have ever seen in our lives. We saw 150,000 people publicly accept Christ.

Hope

To will is also to hope—the willpower to invade the future with a new and a fresh experience. Hope is a strong force. It is a force that determines our destiny. When hope surges within you, by the power of your will, things begin to change. You do not accept the status quo. You do not accept things as they are.

Your will is the determining factor to say, "I am hoping for a better day or a better situation." Your will brings energy into action that causes a change.

At Will

What do the words *at will* mean? They mean an intelligent creature moves and thinks in an uninhibited manner as he desires, wishes, or feels. He has the right and power to do it. He does it "at will." This is a category of greatness, potential life, strength, and vigor that we can hardly imagine.

Do you realize that 90 percent of the world population today cannot function "at will"? They do not have the freedom.

This causes frustration because man is born with a free will. God created him a free moral agent. He is in complete charge of his willfulness; either to follow God or not to follow God, to live peacefully or not to live peacefully. God has permitted him to have this tremendous force of will to be what the Lord has designed and wants him to be.

Possibly man has never yet fathomed the depths of the intelligent will of a human person or the complete will of humankind.

15
The Will of God the Father

———◆◆◆———

What do we truly know about the will of the person of God the Father, who, in divine providence and wisdom, created the will itself?

Jehovah God has a will. He created all the will in the universe. When God created intelligent creatures He set them free through the mighty agency called will.

God's Will in Heaven

In the gospel of Matthew 6:9–10, the disciples asked Jesus to teach them how to pray. He said, *"After this manner therefore pray ye: Our Father...."*

That is remarkable. God is not our boss or our dictator. He is our Father. The father image is a remarkable one.

"...which art in heaven, hallowed be thy name. Thy kingdom come. Thy will be done in earth, as it is in heaven."

The will of God is done in heaven. How can that will be identified here on the face of the earth?

God's Will in Man

God the Father possesses a will. In 1 Thessalonians 5:18 we find these words: *"For this is the will of God in Christ Jesus concerning you."*

God gave a will to all intelligent creatures, which means He gave a part or a portion of Himself. On earth we have the will of God, the will of Christ, the will of the Holy Spirit, the will of angels, and the will of men; there is also the will of the devil and of demons.

God's Will Is Not Difficult

The first thing we must understand is that the will of God for us is not difficult. That will distress some people who say, "My, but the will of God is so hard." It is the devil who speaks things like that.

In Psalm 40:8, David said, *"I delight to do thy will, O my God: yea, thy law is within my heart."*

David had discovered God's will, and he said, *"I delight to do thy will, O my God: yea, thy law is within my heart."* How would one go about seeking to know the will of God the Father?

First, knowing that He is a father, you do not have to scream at Him, crying, "Oh, God, show me Your will!"

When I had three sons at home, if they came screaming downstairs in the morning while I was having a cup of coffee with my wife, saying, "What is your will, Father? What is your will?" I would have said, "Right now, go back to bed and get some rest!"

Possibly God feels that way about some of us sometimes when we start screaming at Him. Knowing the will of God is simple and so easy. All you have to do is understand His Fatherhood.

My three sons, though I do not know exactly where they are at this moment, are in my will because they are my sons. As God's children, we do what He wants us to do because we are His children. You do not have to worry, "Am I in the will of God?" Yes, because you are born into the family. Unless you have violated His will, you are in His will. All Christians are in the will of God, unless they have rebelled against His will. All unsaved people are out of the will of God, for the simple reason that they are in a state of rebellion against God.

God will teach us how to do His will. In Psalm 143:10, it says, *"Teach me to do thy will; for thou art my God* [that is a good confession to make]: *thy spirit is good; lead me into the land of uprightness."* Here we find a man who had come to understand the will of God. He said, *"Teach me to do thy will; for thou art my God: thy spirit is good; lead me into the land of uprightness."*

Romans 12:2 says, *"Be not conformed to this world."* Nonconformity to the world means total dedication— when we say, "Lord, we're going to serve You fully, completely, and absolutely," then our will is subject to the will of God. We are walking in what we call "God's will."

In Ephesians 6:6 Paul said, *"Not with eyeservice, as menpleasers; but as the servants of Christ, doing the will of God from the heart."* That means down within us there is a will, and that will moves through our emotions and minds. We determine, operate, and function in the will of God from an inner source of power that comes to us through the new birth—as a gift from God.

God's Permissive Will

In studying the will we find a remarkable situation—God the Father has a permissive will. He has a strong will that says, "Do this," and He means it. He also has a permissive will. You make the decision, then you ask God to bless it. I must tell you that multiplied millions live in the permissive will of God.

When I was a boy growing up I often lived in the permissive will of my parents—not in their full will, nor in their delighted will. I would want to do something and they would say, "We do not want you to do it." I would say, "I want to do it," and their answer was, "Well, go ahead and do it." Sometimes it brought troubles, sorrows, and problems because my will was not subject to them. The human will is wild until God gets hold of it and makes it subject to His will.

God's Perfect Will

It is God's will that you be saved. It is God's will that you have health. It is not God's will for you to be sick. God's will is for us to be strong right up to the time we go to heaven. Moses was a beautiful example of the will of God. He lived one hundred and twenty years, and the last day he lived he climbed a mountain by himself. From the mountain he beheld the treasures and beauties of God for Israel. Then he gave up the ghost, and the angels took him to heaven.

It is the will of God for you to make quality decisions in your business, your family, and your own life. It is God's will that you be a very successful person upon the face of this earth.

As far as I know, since I was seventeen years of age, I have walked in the will of God. I wanted His will. I subjected my will to His will. I did not go to the Philippines because I wanted to go. I did not come to South Bend, Indiana, to minister because I wanted to. I was born in New Orleans, Louisiana, and would have preferred living in a Southern city. But God's will is to be accomplished. The reason I can teach these things is that I have been comforted by walking in the will of God these many years. By walking in the will of God, I can understand what God's will is concerning me, and what my will is concerning God. It is a resourceful and happy life, a blessed life.

Living in God's Will

We receive what we are through the will of God. First Corinthians 1:1 says, *"Paul, called to be an apostle of Jesus Christ through the will of God."*

Paul knew that he had received apostleship and ministry through the will of God.

That means Paul's will became subservient to the Father's will and he had position in the church through the will of God. Also in 2 Corinthians 1:1 it says, *"Paul, an apostle of Jesus Christ by the will of God."*

All spiritual leadership and position should be according to God's desires and knowledge of human need. We should fit into that. We should be whatever our nation needs the most by the will of God.

The problem that I see in the word *will* is that we have used it so much that we do not know what "will" is. We cannot find the source of it. We cannot find the outflow of it. We are actually laboring in an unknown area.

The will originated in God. It was given to man. If we learn this we will know how to function in the will of God. We must learn to function in the will of God. We must learn to function in a will that has been made new, dedicated, and set apart to carry out the "will of God on earth as it is in heaven."

Thankfulness of God's Will

God's will is that we be thankful. *"In every thing give thanks: for this is the will of God in Christ Jesus concerning you"* (1 Thessalonians 5:18).

God desires thankfulness. It is God's will that you be grateful.

You would be amazed at how many people sit down to eat without giving thanks. Many people go to bed at night without thanking God for the day. Most people begin their days without thanking God for the night.

Also, people receive good things in their lives without saying, "Thank You, God." The will of God concerning you, the Bible says, is that you give thanks to God.

Being Subject to the Will of God

In Matthew 7:21, Jesus said, *"Not every one that saith unto me, Lord, Lord, shall enter into the kingdom of heaven; but he that doeth the will of my Father which is in heaven."*

The will of God has a relationship with your eternal destiny. You cannot just do as you please! You cannot just let your will run riot and expect to reach heaven. Jesus said that what will get you to heaven is doing the will of the Father who is in heaven.

There are people living now whose lives are not subject to the will of God. Those who do as they please are living in their own will and desires. Those people find themselves not in the proper relationship with the Most High God. The will of God the Father is that you know His will and perform it.

Knowing God and His Will

It is the will of God that all men have a keen knowledge of God. *"Who will have all men to be saved, and to come unto the knowledge of the truth"* (1 Timothy 2:4).

It is the will of God that we accept the Great Commission:

> Go ye into all the world, and preach the gospel to every creature. He that believeth and is baptized shall be saved; but he that believeth not shall be damned. And these signs shall follow them that believe; In my name shall they cast out devils.   (Mark 16:15–17)

The will of God is that you and I be pioneers in our generation, delivering the message of truth, power, and eternal salvation throughout the earth.

Your willpower has to rise up within you and say, "I will walk in the will of the Lord!"

16
The Will of Jesus Christ

We have now come to the will of Jesus Christ.

Before Christ was born, He willed to come to earth and be born of the Virgin Mary. His will began before His appearance on earth.

The Lord Jesus possessed divine free will, or as the Son of God, royal free will. The Gospels record that Jesus said, "I will" at least sixty times. Something within Him was a determining factor. Something within Him was a guiding force. It is called will. Jesus exercised what we call "free will." He did not have to do the things He did. He did not have to heal the sick. He did not have to feed the hungry. He had free will.

Jesus Christ went to the cross freely. When Pilate said, "Don't you know that I can kill you?" He said, "No, you cannot do anything unless it is the will of God."

Jesus said, "Don't you realize I can call legions of angels to set me free?" He willfully went to the cross.

The will of Jesus gave Him a source of energy to achieve world redemption. He willed to save the world. By this will He drove His body to the cross. He drove His spirit to the cross by His willpower. Jesus said in Luke 22:42, *"Father, if thou be willing, remove this cup from* me: *nevertheless not my will, but thine, be done."* Jesus was living in the will of the Father.

Christ revealed God's will in His life. The beginning of this revealing of the will of God is found in Luke 2:49. Jesus was speaking to His own parents, *"How is it that ye sought me? wist ye not that I must be about my Father's business?"* When Jesus was twelve years old, He wanted His parents to know there was a will stronger than His will.

Christ was demonstrating His will at twelve years of age. I do not think you can be too young to function and work in the will of God for your life.

Jesus desired that His own will would not be performed. He knew that the Father in heaven had a will greater, more magnificent, and more wonderful than the will of man. Jesus chose that His will would coordinate with the will of the Father. He knew that He had come to perform the will of the Father on the earth. John 5:30 says, *"I can of mine own self do nothing: as I hear, I judge: and my judgment is just; because I seek not mine own will, but the will of the Father which hath sent me."*

That is about as strong a verse as you can find in the Bible. It means Christ had a will, and could have opposed the plan of God, but He said, "I will not seek My will, but the will of the Father who sent Me."

Evidently the superior will of the universe is in the Father. Doing the will of God is the greatest achievement on the face of this earth. We must seek the will of God. We must find the will of God; then we must coordinate it with our will. We should not say, "I do not want to do this, but I will do it anyway." That is not what God wants at all.

The perfect will of God flows out of us spontaneously, like an artesian well flowing with living water.

God desires that you have His ultimate will coming joyfully out of your heart as Christ had.

Jesus Christ entered human history to teach mankind how to perform God's will. That is the reason He was born. Hebrews 10:7-10 says,

> *Then said I, Lo, I come (in the volume of the book it is written of me,) to do thy will, O God. Above when he said, Sacrifice and offering and burnt offerings and offering for sin thou wouldest not, neither hadst pleasure therein; which are offered by the law; then said he, Lo, I come to do thy will, O God. He taketh away the first, that he may establish the second. By the which will we are sanctified through the offering of the body of Jesus Christ once for all.*

Christ entered human history to teach mankind—you and I—how we can perform the will of God.

Jesus Lived by God's Will

When you survey the life of Christ, you can see that after His birth in Bethlehem, life in Nazareth, and traveling about all over that nation doing good and bringing healing, love and blessing to those people, He was performing not human will, but a divine mission. *"I am come that they might have life, and that they might have it more abundantly"* (John 10:10). He said in John 9:4, *"I must work the works of him that sent me, while it is day: the night cometh, when no man can work."* Jesus had instilled deep within Him a desire to perform only the will of God the Father.

Christ revealed a beautiful relationship of His will in the area of people who are sick. Matthew 8:3 says, *"And Jesus put forth his hand, and touched him, saying, I will; be thou clean. And immediately his leprosy was cleansed."*

Here was a man who missed Jesus. He came up to Him and said, "Master, I know that You can heal me if You will." He believed in Jesus' power but not His love. He spoke in unbelief. Jesus turned and said, *"I will; be thou clean."* The human will was desire. The divine will poured forth its life.

Direction of Jesus' Will

What functioned in directing the will in Jesus? First, I would say His love. Christ came to reveal a divine attitude. God is love, so He came to reveal God. The will in the life of Jesus functioned through a spirit-life within Him called love.

Will can also be compassion. In His will, Christ suffered with mankind! He hurt with mankind. He cared for mankind! This is compassion. So His will functioned in compassion and love.

Christ was the moving, walking, talking, living will of God, and He demonstrated that will.

Christ demonstrated the will of the Father in His labors. He slept at night on the ground—He had no bed. He walked many miles over rough terrain—He had no animal to ride. There were times He was hungry. There were times He was thirsty. He did not have to do that, but He willed to do it. He desired within Himself to do it.

In this area His mind could have said, "Do it." His emotions could have said, "Do it." The will could have stopped and balked. On the other hand, His will could say, "Do it." His emotions could say, "Oh, it's too hard." His mind could say, "Hey, this is too much work." But His will would win because the will is the strongest force in the human person.

Jesus demonstrated the great will of heaven, the will of God the Father. He revealed it through His attitude of life, love, and labors.

Christ revealed what will means down on the inside of Christians, rising up in strength, blessing, and health.

One of the greatest aspects of Jesus' demonstration of the will of God was in His forgiveness. He willed to forgive people. It is divine to forgive. Christ harbored no grudges, hates, or unforgiveness. When Judas came to give Him the kiss of betrayal, Jesus said, "Friend, what can I do for you?" He knew what he was going to do. He had already gone through the prayer in the garden. When Peter cursed and said that he had never heard of Jesus and did not know Him, Jesus said, "Call Peter back, and I'll forgive him." He would have forgiven Judas, if Judas had come and asked for forgiveness, but he could not come.

Will is demonstrated when you are a baby. The wildest tantrums are willpower. It is not mental or emotional, but willpower. We often talk about "having to break a person's will." I do not think that is a good word; you do not want to break anything—you want it to flow in God.

Jesus came to this earth to demonstrate that a human person could walk this earth and yet be in the will of God. Christ said, "I will be the perfect example of living and working in the will of God."

17
The Will of the Holy Spirit

◆●◆

*J*esus said He would send another Comforter. *"And I will pray the Father, and he shall give you another Comforter, that he may abide with you for ever"* (John 14:16).

That meant the Holy Spirit would be a comforter.

Jesus said that He (the Holy Spirit) would teach you all things. *"For the Holy Ghost shall teach you in the same hour what ye ought to say"* (Luke 12:12).

Christ said the Holy Spirit will remind you of the things that are past.

Jesus said that He will guide you. This speaks of a person, not of an "it," or an influence. So we are dealing with the will of the *person* of the Holy Spirit.

In John 3:8 the Lord Jesus said, *"The wind* [speaking of the Holy Spirit] *bloweth where it listeth* [the Holy Spirit blows where He wills]*, and thou hearest the sound thereof, but canst not tell whence it cometh, and whither it goeth: so is every one that is born of the Spirit."*

Christ was teaching a very learned man named Nicodemus who came to Him to understand the way of salvation. He was trying to show him that there is a place in God where the Holy Spirit does what He wants to do.

The Holy Spirit's Will in the Old Testament

The first place in recorded Scripture where we see activity of the Holy Spirit is in Genesis 1:2. It is remarkable that the first page and second verse of the Bible shows the activity of the Holy Spirit. It says, *"And the earth was without form, and void; and darkness was upon the face of the deep. And the Spirit of God moved upon the face of the waters."*

This is the recorded volitional decision of the third person of the Holy Trinity. It was the act of bringing cosmos, beauty, and loveliness out of chaos. The earth was without form and void. God was involved in His creative masterpiece, and the Holy Spirit moved to help Him. The Spirit of God moved on the face of the waters, and cosmos came out of the chaos. The dynamic will of the Holy Spirit challenged the condition, succeeded, and brought it into fruition. It is the first record of the functioning of the Holy Spirit.

The Holy Spirit has moved since the beginning of time upon this earth and in eternity, but in these last days we are living in what is called the Dispensation of the Holy Spirit. You and I should know more about the Holy Spirit than they did in those days because this is His dispensation.

Jesus said, "If I go away, I will send Him unto you." The Holy Spirit is special to us, and we should understand His will. His will is the same as the will of the Lord Jesus. The Holy Spirit is absolutely, completely, wonderfully, and gloriously submitted unto the Lord Jesus Christ, our Savior.

Genesis 6:3 says, *"And the LORD said, My spirit shall not always strive with man."*

Here we see the Holy Spirit, by His own will, volitionally, created limits in which He would beg or persuade man to walk in the ways and commandments of Elohim, the mighty God. God said, "I want you to live right; I want you to live well. I sent My Holy Spirit to guide and to direct you." Volitionally, the Holy Spirit said, "I will not always beg, I will not always strive, I will not always urge men to serve God." No wonder the Bible says in Ephesians 4:30, *"Grieve not the holy Spirit of God."* He can be grieved. Maybe that is also in the area of will, because if a man does not will to grieve others, he will not grieve them.

In the first instance, we find the Holy Spirit bringing cosmos to the earth. In the second instance, we find Him pleading with men, and volitionally saying, "I will not always do this; I'm doing it now, but I will not always do this."

The Holy Spirit possesses the willpower of saying His grace and help would go only so far, and no farther.

The Holy Spirit's Will in the New Testament

> But a certain man named Ananias, with Sapphira his wife, sold a possession, and kept back part of the price, his wife also being privy to it, and brought a certain part, and laid it, at the apostles' feet. But Peter said, Ananias, why hath Satan filled thine heart to lie to the Holy Ghost, and to keep back part of the price of the land? (Acts 5:1–3)

The Holy Spirit willed capital punishment upon Ananias and Sapphira for lying to deity, to the Most High God. He knew everything; they could not lie to Him.

This incident brought great respect to God and the church in Jerusalem.

I have witnessed the judgment of the Holy Spirit in my own lifetime. I conducted a meeting in a town in Arkansas. I especially urged a young man to give his heart to the Lord Jesus. The Holy Spirit was tugging at his will. There were tears in his eyes, but he would not do it. He said, "No, I will not do it." He became very angry in church; he abused his sister because she became a Christian, and he led her out of the church roughly. He said, "Come out of this place. You do not need this kind of religion."

A couple of days later he was plowing in a field when lightning came out of a clear sky, hit him, and drove his body into the ground. They found his shoe thirty yards away. It was completely torn, as if someone had taken a knife and cut it to pieces.

You cannot forsake God and get away with it. The Holy Spirit has a ministry of bringing people to God.

The Holy Spirit wills to guide the church. The Bible says that as the disciples were fasting and praying, *"the Holy Ghost said, Separate me Barnabas and Saul for the work whereunto I have called them"* (Acts 13:2).

The Holy Spirit volitionally endorsed the missionaries to go forth. They were sent by the strength, power, and guidance of the Holy Spirit. That is what God desires in His church today. The Holy Spirit wants to guide the church. The church in rebellion to the Holy Spirit can get into big trouble, sorrow, heartache, and big problems by grieving Him. He is a person, and He has a will.

The will of the Holy Spirit is to carry out the desires of the Father. His will is to fulfill whatever the Father says will be done. His will is to carry out the words and desires of the Lord Jesus. His will is to enrich the church. The will of the Holy Spirit is to anoint. It is the will of the Holy Spirit to come upon us. It is the will of the Holy Spirit to come on the total church. It is the will of the Holy Spirit to come upon missions.

You say, "Can't the Holy Spirit perform His will without me?" The Holy Spirit will not use you against your will. There are denominations that do not desire the Holy Spirit to work; they are afraid of Him. It is a sad situation to be living in the Dispensation of the Holy Spirit and be afraid for Him to operate, function, and do the things He has been sent to do.

We all need to say, "Holy Spirit, my will is flowing with Your will because Your will flows with the Father, and I am flowing with the Father through You."

The Holy Spirit wills to anoint people. The Holy Spirit grants gifts to people. First Corinthians 12:11 says, *"But all these worketh that one and the selfsame Spirit, dividing to every man severally as he will."*

18
The Will of Angels

———◆◆◆———

You may have thought that angels can do as they please. This is not true. Angels have volitional powers just like you. Some angels have transgressed just like humans, because they have a will.

Angels Were Created with Will

In Judges 13:16, *"And the angel of the LORD said unto Manoah, Though thou detain me, I will not eat of thy bread."* This angel was showing Manoah that he had a will. He could will to do this or not to do that.

Angels are created beings. They have no navel. They are not born of a woman. *"In the beginning God created the heaven and the earth"* (Genesis 1:1).

Almighty God, in His select wisdom, created angels as servants and messengers. They were made for Him and possess willpower. They do not have to serve God. They may serve God or rebel against Him.

Angels are superintelligent creatures, beyond man's comprehension. They have knowledge of two worlds, the spirit world and the physical world. They are two-world creatures. Sometimes the wall of partition is broken down, and you can see angels. Angels can talk to God and with man. God designed angels and gave

them superpowers of decision about special factors. He
did this because He wants to merit their love.

Angels Will to Worship

A beautiful look into the angelic world is recorded
in Isaiah 6:1–4,

> *In the year that king Uzziah died I saw also the Lord*
> *sitting upon a throne, high and lifted up, and his train*
> *filled the temple. Above it stood the seraphims: each*
> *one had six wings; with twain he covered his face, and*
> *with twain he covered his feet, and with twain he did*
> *fly. And one cried unto another, and said, Holy, holy,*
> *holy, is the* LORD *of hosts: the whole earth is full of his*
> *glory. And the posts of the door moved at the voice of*
> *him that cried, and the house was filled with smoke.*

Here we find angels in worship before the throne
crying, *"Holy, holy, holy, is the* LORD *of hosts."* They
were worshipping volitionally. They wanted to worship. They liked to worship, because they enjoyed it.
They smile big and sing magnificently before the Lord.
They did this with their will—they willed to do it.

Angels Will to Protect

Psalm 34:7 says, *"The angel of the* LORD *encampeth*
round about them that fear him, and delivereth them." An
angel by his willpower protects good, righteous, and
holy people.

I could relate stories of how angels have protected
missionaries. Wicked men have tried to destroy missionaries on the field, and the next day they would
say, "We would like to see the army that was around

your compound last night. We saw men ten feet tall walking all around your place, and we were afraid to hurt you."

If God would open your spiritual eyes, you might be amazed at what is there, and thank God for His protecting power by His angels.

Angels Will to Harvest Souls

The angels will bring in the final spiritual harvest. This reaches into the future, but it shows you that the angels have a will to do things for God.

In Matthew 12:39 we read, *"But he answered and said unto them, An evil and adulterous generation seeketh after a sign; and there shall no sign be given to it, but the sign of the prophet Jonas."* Jesus continues by saying the angels will bring in the harvest of God.

Angelic Will and Prophecy

Angels brought prophecy to man. Daniel 9:21 says,

> *Yea, whiles I was speaking in prayer, even the man Gabriel, whom I had seen in the vision at the beginning, being caused to fly swiftly, touched me about the time of the evening oblation.*

Gabriel was sent from God. This means that he had a will, and he was obedient.

Angelic Will and Humans

Angels can be entertained by humans. Hebrews 13:2 says, *"Be not forgetful to entertain strangers: for thereby*

some have entertained angels unawares." Abraham was
unaware that the visitors who came to his tent were
angels. He thought they were regular people. He made
a feast for them but later discovered the angels had a
message for him from God.

My mother believed we entertained angels in our
home, and she gave reasons for that belief.

Angels have been, and are, very influential persons who function by their will. They will to do what
God asks them to do.

19
The Will of Demons

◆●◆

*D*emons have intelligent wills. They know and understand what they do. They do what they do very deliberately. Many times there is a battle of wills. This was true not only in the Lord Jesus' battle of wills against the devil, but it is also true in our lives. There is a battle of wills when the devil says, "Do this" and you say, "No." Your mind can say, "I want to do this." Your emotions say, "Oh, that's nice." When your will says, "No," it is finished.

Your will is the strongest part of your soulical being. You must learn how to yield it to Christ. You must know that it has to be renewed like the mind. In order for the will to be what Jesus wants it to be, it has to be born again, along with the rest of your soulical being.

Willpower Created Demons

An amazing area of willpower centers around the devil and demons. They became what they are because of their will. God did not make them that way. They became that way through their will. Until you realize there is a battle of will between you and the devil, between you and the world, and between you and the flesh, you may lose every battle. When you know, then you will be well-armed to be a winner. Demons know both the positive and negative aspects of the power of the will. They knew what it was like to follow God, live for God, and sing in the heavens. They heard Lucifer say, "I will promote myself above the throne of God. I will make myself like the Most High." When the devil tried that through the power of his will, he lost his divine relationship with God. In Isaiah 14:12–14, it says,

> *How art thou fallen from heaven, O Lucifer, son of the morning! how art thou cut down to the ground, which didst weaken the nations! For thou hast said in thine heart, I will ascend into heaven, I will exalt my throne above the stars of God: I will sit also upon the mount of the congregation, in the sides of the north: I will ascend above the heights of the clouds; I will be like the most High.*

Lucifer is history's masterpiece of arrogance. Nowhere in the universe will you find arrogance equal to his. Here was a created being who, through his own will, said, "I will be greater than the One who created me." Created ones cannot be as great as their Creator. It is not possible. A wristwatch will never be as great as the man who made it. A watch can keep good time and do a lot of things, but it cannot be as great as the one who created it. You are a person created by God, and you can never be as great as God. He created you; He designed you; He made you. It is not intelligent to think that one day you will be greater than God.

This archangel named Lucifer made five astounding statements of will. He was moving forth not in taste, emotion, and not even intellect. He was moving in willpower.

Demonic Will in Eden

The second step in the battle of the wills took place in the Garden of Eden. Satan deceived man in their first encounter. Man was seduced in the Garden by Satan's willful fall. Adam knew that it was God's will that he should not eat of the tree, yet he willed to eat the fruit.

He willfully decided to be someone else when he could have been like God. In the first encounter of will on earth, Satan trapped man by his will, and caused man to leave the will of God and serve the will of the devil.

Demonic Will Today

How does the devil try to hurt believers today? In John 10:10 Jesus said, *"The thief* [or the devil] *cometh not, but for to steal, and to kill, and to destroy."*

When the devil comes against you, he wants to do three things. He comes to steal from you. That is what he did to Eve and Adam in the Garden. He stole their willpower and desire to walk with God.

Not only does the devil steal, but he kills and destroys. The devil is a killer. The Bible says he was a murderer from the beginning. He is a destroyer of life. The only way he can do it is by breaking down your will; then you will be like Eve. His system has always been the same. It is a battle of wills.

You will have a battle of will every day. At church time there is a battle of the wills. "Will I go to church or will I stay home?" It is a battle of will inside you. It is not a battle of your emotions. It is not a battle of your mind. It is a battle of the will. If you do not obey the divine and spiritual part of your will, you will be like Satan. The devil seeks to hurt and destroy your will if he possibly can.

20
The Will of Humankind

◆●◆

God created Adam. He was the first person, first human, first earthling. God created him from the earth, so when man dies he goes back to the earth. He was not created by mixing some chemical acids.

Three-Dimensional Man

God created man, a three-dimensional personality. Neither psychology nor psychiatry realize this, and humanism will never understand it at all.

Everything in this universe that was initially perfect is indelibly stamped with a three. God is Father, Son, and Holy Spirit—the three function as one.

Man is a spirit, soul, and body—functioning as one.

The will is one-third of the human soulical personality. The soul is one-third of the total personality of the total person. Your soulical parts consist of your mind, emotions, and will. This is how you relate to other humans.

When God created man and placed him in Eden, He said, "There is one tree here that belongs to Me. The other trees and their fruit belong to you."

Every home is the same. The father says, "This is mine." Mama says, "This is mine, and son, this is yours." Inevitably the little boy wants Papa's, Mama's, and his. This was the problem in the Garden of Eden. God said, "We are partners. I built the whole scheme of things. I'll put you in charge; but one tree, the Tree of the Knowledge of Good and Evil, you may not touch." That tree was a test of character for Adam. It was up to Adam to operate positively in his will to obey God, or negatively to disobey Him.

First Corinthians 15:45 says, *"And so it is written, The first man Adam was made a living soul; the last Adam was made a quickening spirit."* This Scripture describes the difference between Adam of the Garden of Eden and Jesus Christ.

You and I are naturally the seed of Adam. We are supernaturally the seed of Jesus Christ, the seed of God. The Bible says that when you believe upon the Lord you become the son of God. As soon as you believe you are a son of God, you move into another realm, and your total abilities, spirit, soul, and body, relate to God and spiritual things. When your will is obedient to God, the emotional and mental areas of your life will fall in line because the will has power to discipline.

The will first has to be regenerated. Through Adam we become living souls, but in Christ we become quickening spirits. We are twice sons; we are sons of Adam naturally, and we are sons of the Spirit supernaturally. As sons of God, our wills have been cleansed, purified, and renewed.

The Bible is the solitary source of knowledge regarding the mystery of the inner workings of the human person. Philosophers do not know this. They search everywhere except the true source to find out about man.

> *For the word of God is quick, and powerful, and sharper than any twoedged sword, piercing even to the dividing asunder of soul and spirit, and of the joints and marrow, and is a discerner of the thoughts and intents of the heart.* (Hebrews 4:12)

Human Life Dominated by Will

The human will begins to function at the time of birth. You may not have realized this, but doctors know. During labor the baby assists in delivery. He brings himself out.

In childhood when a child says, "No, no, no," he is exercising willpower, not physical or emotional power.

At the time of spiritual conversion and the born-again experience, a person comes into a tremendous situation of will. He wills to receive Christ as his Savior and becomes a new creature in Christ Jesus. His process of will is changed.

Will is also involved in your receiving the Holy Spirit. There are some people who have the will to be saved but do not have the will to go further in God. Their will ceases at the point of salvation. The Bible explicitly tells us in 1 John that there are three witnesses to God in the earth. They are the blood, the water, and the Spirit. Some people stop at the blood. Some stop at the blood and water. Some get all the way through to the Spirit. When the three function, you will be what God desires you to be.

Not only is the will powerful in receiving the Holy Spirit, but also in operating in the gifts and ministries of the Holy Spirit. Willpower is there. If you do not will to accept it, it will not work. If you do not will to have them, they will not operate. The will is a source of desire. It is a source of hope.

The human will is a decision-maker. It is a willful activity. A non-decision is also a decision. When your will refuses to function and make a decision, it makes a decision.

An unconscious decision is the fruit of the will. When you do things unconsciously, your will has been disciplined to act under certain circumstances and influences. Therefore, an unconscious decision is the fruit of the human will.

It was Eve's will that caused her to fall. It was not Eve's body—her five senses. It was her will. When the tempter Satan said, "Listen. You will be great and you will be equal with God if you eat this," her will within her said, "I will be as great as God. I will be like the Most High." It was her will that caused her downfall.

Will Is a Gift

The human will is a gift from God. The greatest experience of human achievement is performing the will of God. The human will is immortal. You will have it after this life. You will keep your will in eternity, and those who go to heaven will possess the will to serve God and enjoy heaven. Those who go to hell will have a will.

Sovereign Will

The human will is sovereign. God will not violate it. He created you and made you a responsible person. You cannot blame God for the actions of your will. You are the one who does the driving. God will not stop your will. If He did you would not be a human anymore. You would be a broken creature without a will.

Satan cannot violate your will, because he does not have power to do it. God made the human will so strong that Satan has to ask you to grant him your will. You determine your decisions, and then your guardian angel can act for you. You have to stress your own willpower and move in a certain direction before your angel can act on your behalf. Angels are not permitted to control human will. Only you can control your own will.

Demons seek to control your destiny by your will. In their attempt to control the human will or to weaken the will, demons can make sin attractive and desirable. They try to break down the willpower by saying, "This won't hurt you. That won't hurt you. This won't take you to hell." They seek to break down your will to serve the Lord Jesus. Demons use deceit and trickery against the human will.

The human will, to be protected, must live in the Word of God and worship of God. It must be humble before the Lord. Then the human soul will certainly be victorious.

When you say, "Thy will be done," it is a spiritual act and not an Adamic act. Adam actually put his will against God's will. First Corinthians 15:22 says, *"For as in Adam all die, even so in Christ shall all be made alive."*

Adam deliberately, volitionally, and willfully rebelled against God.

The Lord Jesus Christ volitionally submitted His will to God the Father. That is the difference between the two.

The Redeemed Will

In the new life of the Second Adam, we see the strategies of spiritual life and warfare. We are taught from the Bible about the Lord Jesus. We are taught by the Holy Spirit. We learn how to battle successfully against the devil in the world of will. We also learn how to worship God in the world of will. There is a real danger in the lack of teaching. There has been little teaching on will.

The unconverted human will of a child, who screams, kicks, and yells, exercises uncontrolled and undisciplined willpower. The child is not using his mind. There is no pain in the child's body, yet he wills to scream uncontrollably. He wants attention. This child must learn to bring his will to God.

The converted man is the opposite. His will and total soulical parts had an amazing and miraculous change at conversion. The rebellion against God ceased to exist.

Discerning Will

The supreme message of this hour is the comprehension of what is God's will, man's will, and the devil's will!

The devil wants to take us all to Armageddon and kill us.

Man does not know what he wants to do. He flutters around like a butterfly. He thinks he wants all kinds of sensual accomplishments. They do not satisfy him. Man is an immortal creature and cannot fully be satisfied without loving, praising, and honoring God. Only through the spirit can man know the spiritual reality of God's will.

Most people have no idea about God's will. We say "will" so quickly until we do not even hear it, but we need to say it a lot slower. W-I-L-L is so important. It is impossible to have spiritual development and maturity without an understanding of the different functions of the human will. There are many Christians today who know the Lord Jesus Christ, yet live in the soulical part of their will that is in rebellion.

Until a Christian can differentiate between God's will and his own will, he will most likely be living in the lower realm of his own will and not in the spiritual realm—the upper realm of God's will. It is impossible to continually walk in God's will until we know what God's will is. To the natural man it is a mystery. In Matthew 11:25 Jesus said, *"I thank thee, O Father, Lord of heaven and earth, because thou hast hid these things from the wise and prudent, and hast revealed them unto babes."* You and I know a truth others do not know. We understand things about the human person others do not understand. We recognize that man is not just clay and air, but that he is divine and mysteries such as the human mind, emotions, and will were planted within him by God.

Doing God's Will

"Wherefore be ye not unwise, but understanding what the will of the Lord is" (Ephesians 5:17). What is God's will in your natural life on this earth? God has a plan for your life dominated by will. He would like for you to let that will be strong in Him and in His great power.

"Not with eyeservice, as menpleasers; but as the servants of Christ, doing the will of God from the heart" (Ephesians 6:6). Man can do as he pleases. God is not going to overwhelm him. If you do not will an act to be a certain way, it will never be that way. God is asking for a will submitted to Him. It is the will of God for the Gospel to be preached in the entire world. If you wish to do the

will of God, accept the challenge of the Great Commission. Your mind and emotions may not want to, but your will is the dominating factor. It is your will that can cause you to be the person that God wants you to be.

Man worships by his will. In Matthew 6:10, Jesus said to pray, *"Thy kingdom come. Thy will be done in earth, as it is in heaven."*

One day the Lord Jesus will reign for a thousand years upon this earth and perform the will of God. The earth will function as God intended it to in the first place. Christians will reign with Him and perform the will of God.

If you will say today, "God, I am interested in performing Your will in my life, family, church, and country," the will of God will be revealed and accomplished.

21
Imagination—The Hidden Force of Human Destiny

◆●◆

I was born in New Orleans, Louisiana. I lived in Laurel, Mississippi; Mobile, Alabama; and Panama City, Florida. Almost everyone I knew was poor, yet my father usually owned a car, and we lived in an average house. He worked in the machine shops of ship and railroad yards.

Though we were poor, I was endowed with a wild imagination. For example, a man named Mr. Gaddis owned a men's clothing store that catered to the well-to-do people of the city. He was a member of the Pines Country Club. I got to know him by being his golf caddy. I wasn't very big—about as tall as his golf bag—but he liked me. He would come to the club and say, "Is Lester here?"

Often I would fantasize: "One day I am going to own a store like Mr. Gaddis." I could see my store and myself standing and watching the people enter. I had imagination!

God redirected my imagination. My imagination created images of my future and destiny and the destiny of anyone I touched.

I would see men like Billy Sunday, the famous sawdust-trail evangelist, who came to our city and built a wooden tabernacle that seated several thousand people. Without a PA system he would speak to thousands.

At home I would take off my coat, lay it down, jump on a bed, then on a chair—I was Billy Sunday!

Billy Sunday would leave the platform and run down into the audience to preach. I never saw a preacher do this, and I thought it was great. I could see myself doing it.

I do not remember ever hearing a sermon on imagination. Yet the imagination is a hidden force that relates to human destiny.

Imagination is a creative ability that you should permit to function. However, do not let it become a time-waster. You can imagine that you are rich, but you cannot buy goods at the store with imagination. You cannot buy a new automobile with imagination.

Imagination is a starter. It is a prompter. If you use it for the reason God gave it to you, it is a very valuable asset and produces success.

Have imagination, but do not stop there. It is like a man who wants a house and the architect draws a picture of it. He says, "I like the house." He does not have the house; he has the image of what it can become.

Harness your imagination. Direct your imagination. Put it to work for your total life.

God wants you to use all the resources He has put within you.

22

I Have Imagination

———————— ◆●◆ ————————

*I*magination gives birth to empires, fortunes, beautiful buildings, lovely bridges across waters, and beautiful automobiles. Imagination is a tremendous force. It is creative.

According to Jesus, every imagination of the heart will be revealed one day. This shows the importance of imagination. All great events and achievements have their base in imagination.

Imagination can grow. It can be fed. It can be taught. It can increase. Imagination can be guided. You have full control over your personal imagination.

In 1 Chronicles 28:9, David, a senior statesman, spoke to his son,

> *And thou, Solomon my son, know thou the God of thy father, and serve him with a perfect heart and with a willing mind: for the Lord searcheth all hearts, and understandeth all the imaginations of the thoughts: if thou seek him, he will be found of thee; but if thou forsake him, he will cast thee off for ever.*

What awesome advice! David told Solomon, "I am an older man and getting ready to leave this earth. My son, I want you to know the God of your own father. I want you to serve Him with a perfect heart."

David said, "God knows the imaginations of the heart." Some people say, "As long as I just fantasize sin, it is not wrong." Jesus said He would judge man by what he desired to do. Jesus said when a man lusted after a woman he had already committed adultery.

You must learn the source of your imagination, and the guidance available to your imaginative propensities.

Imagination changes lives, communities, families, and the world in which we live.

God understands all imaginations. He understands what functions inside your brain. That is where imagination originates, in thoughts. God sees not just the deed, as anybody can see. God sees the thought that produces the action.

Until a person can correct and control his thought life, he cannot correct his real life of actions. We must learn to discipline our thought life before we can discipline our hands and feet.

I have imagination. Imagination is the hidden force of human potential!

23
The Birth of Human Imagination

◆◆◆

*T*he human person is so wonderfully and mysteriously made by God that science will never completely understand the intricacies of the human personality.

Imagination is one of the sources of life the Creator gave to humanity. In the birth of the human imagination, we witness the genius of the Almighty.

At the beginning of the Bible, we observe the potential of imagination. Through Adam's rebellion, man turned imagination into a negative structure rather than a positive one. Man used the power and dignity of imagination in destructive action.

The period before the Flood is called the antediluvian age. We discover in Genesis 6:5, *"And God saw that the wickedness of man was great in the earth, and that every imagination of the thoughts of his heart was only evil continually."*

After Noah is the postdiluvian period. The Bible says in Genesis 11:6, *"And the LORD said, Behold, the people is one, and they have all one language; and this they begin to do: and now nothing will be restrained from them, which they have imagined to do."*

What an amazing situation!

God said that because of the unity of the people by language, the forces of imagination could bring into being anything they imagined to do. That means your powers of imagination are unlimited. Every intricate development in science first begins in imagination, then grows into reality.

That is powerful! If you can imagine it, you can do it! Your abilities are really not limited to your education. Your abilities are limited to your imagination. If you can see it, you can bring it into being. In our daily contact with people we often hear some say, "Just imagine!" They mean, "It is almost unbelievable, but evidently it is true."

You have heard people say, "Can you imagine that?" They mean, "Can your mind expand to receive and accept what seems to be impossible?"

Inside a person a force goes into operation. It creates an image that says, "I can do that; though I have not trained to do it, I can learn to do it."

Human imagination spans the past, crosses the present, and predicts the future. You live in the midst of great world imagery.

What Is Imagination?

The human imagination is a function of the conscious mind. It is not from your subliminal mind or unconscious mind, nor is it your nocturnal, nighttime, dreamworld mind.

Imagination is a deliberate action. You call it into being. It often is a fulfillment of hidden desires that want to be expressed. A little girl imagines that she is a mother, because she has a hidden desire to one day be a mother.

Reach into your world of imagination and bring to fruition the inner desires of the total human person. Imagination is deeply related to what is inside you looking for fulfillment. Imagination and fulfillment flow together. Imagination comes out of the world of hope and faith, a projected image waiting to enter the world of reality.

An evolutionist would say this power of imagination grew in man. I do not believe that. I believe God created imagination and gave it to man. Maybe people before the Flood like Adam, Enoch, and Noah had greater powers of imagination than anyone else has ever had. I believe imagination is on the decrease rather than on the increase. It was created for man to use here on earth. There will be no imagination in heaven; there will be only fulfillment. Man's wildest imaginations cannot conceive what God has prepared for him in heaven.

God endowed man with creativity. Everything that has been made by man on the face of this earth was first conceived in the world of imagination before it came into the world of reality.

Adam and Eve were the first to use their imagination, just as they were conscious that they were responsible for the decisions they made. You are responsible for the things you imagine, because it is a deliberate action of a human person. If you permit yourself to imagine wrong, the devil helps you go deeper into wrong imaginations. If you wish to imagine right, the Bible, God, Jesus, and the angels will help you to move into the right and correct imagination world.

Imagination is the power to conceive and give expression to images and dreams that can be moved from the world of imagination into the material, mundane world.

Imagination in itself has no real existence except in the mind. It has no evidence to produce. It is in a world that cannot be seen or heard. It has to come out of your heart in order for you to understand all the things you have imagined.

What we are talking about is not new and novel; it has been with man always and needs to be taught clearly so that everyone will understand why they do certain things. Genesis 3:6 says,

> *And when the woman saw that the tree was good for food, and that it was pleasant to the eyes, and a tree to be desired to make one wise, she took of the fruit thereof, and did eat, and gave also unto her husband with her; and he did eat.*

Satan brought Eve close to the tree and said, "Eve, look at this tree." Eve saw the fruit of that tree. This was a natural, physical situation altogether. She had eye contact with it.

Inside herself Eve believed the fruit to be delicious. That takes imagination! You do not know apple pie is good until you bite into it. It might look good, but that does not make it taste good. If the cook used salt rather than sugar, you would have a crazy-tasting mess instead of a delicious pie. It may look as good as any other apple pie, but it would be salty instead of sweet.

You can pass by the window of a store or a bakery and see something that looks really good, like freshly made cakes. You can say, "Yum, I'd like to have a bite of that." But in our modern world today, they make display goods out of plastic. It only looks delicious!

Eve conceived within her mental powers that what she saw with her eyes would also be delicious to her taste. They are two different functions, seeing and tasting. Eve had no evidence that the fruit was delicious.

Eve said, "It is pleasant to my eyes. I am sure it will be pleasant to my taste." Then Eve went a step further.

She believed Lucifer, who was talking to her, that this tree also had a strange power. The fruit would make her wise.

That is another world. We leave the apple pie world and go into a world of intelligence—apple pie would make you wise.

Eve had eaten this fruit inside her world of imagination, and now it was not only good for her lips, but she was believing from her brain that it was good. You see what imagination can do for you? Eve hit a whole world of unreality. You do not eat fruit for brain food. In Eve's fanciful world she had gotten into what she said, "If I eat this fruit, I'll be smarter than Adam. That's an achievement."

No doubt a great battle surged within Eve. Satan's deception went farther and said, "And you shall be like God!"

Eve had seen God walk in the Garden in the evening with Adam, and she knew Him. Her imagination was the key force that caused the situation to come into fruition.

We must remember that imagination was created for man. God wants you to turn that power, that force, into something big, good, and wonderful!

24
Creative Imagination

◆●◆

*I*magination is the hidden force of human destiny. It is a tremendous power.

Imagination Unlimited

Proverbs 23:7 says, *"For as he thinketh in his heart, so is he."*

As a man thinks!

With creative imagination, you actually create your own destiny. You can create your own well-being. You can create whatever you are. The Word of God specifically teaches us that as a person thinks or imagines, he is!

Creative imagination is positive. Since there is a positive, there has to be a negative. Imagination can create both good and evil. The same instrument inside can work either way.

Imagination is an unlimited quality. You can build upon it. You can excite it. It has many remarkable areas in which it can move. Imagination is governed by set laws. If you abuse it, then it becomes a negative force; but if you support and strengthen it in the things that are good, then imagination is the hidden force of human destiny.

The Law of Imagination

I believe that within every human, there is the potential of becoming whatever can be conceived in the mind or imagination. It is also possible to bring your imaginations into fruition, or reality.

Humans once imagined that they could fly. The Wright brothers brought it into being.

Humans once imagined that they could see inside a person. X rays brought it into being.

If you are a spiritual person your potential in imagination is good, holy, and creative; it is God-ordained. Your imagination gives birth to new worlds to conquer and new blessings to receive.

Imagination can cause you to act—new buildings to build, new crusades for souls, new countries to reach, new gifts of the Holy Spirit to be directed toward you.

In the positive, one can observe that creative imagination is responsible for the masterpieces of humanity. Somebody imagined the Great Wall of China. Someone had to imagine the Colossus at Rhodes before there could be a Colossus. Someone had to imagine the glorious temple at Jerusalem before there could be the Temple of the Most High that Solomon built worth hundreds of millions of dollars.

Great imaginations create beautiful music. Music is the imagination of the soul. The great masters brought music from their inner being to their outer being, and made it a part of the world of knowledge.

The same is true in literature. Before you can produce a book you have to visualize the material.

Maybe you have never used your imagination, but within you there is the spirit and power of creating images. This force creates the same thing through your faculties and use of your hands, mouth, or pen. You bring into being what you have imagined.

Then there is the art world. Michaelangelo had to see the Last Judgment before he could paint it on the Sistine Chapel ceiling. He had to visualize the multitude of colors. He had to see how big to paint God, and how big the devil should be. He placed emperors, popes, and all kinds of people in the painting. He had to see the total picture before he could create it and bring it into being.

All of this human delight began in a world of imagination. Then it emerged to be seen and appreciated.

Your imagination is a force, a power of human destiny. Understand what it is, and guide it into the channels for which God intended and ordained it.

Imagination in engineering brought the wheel into reality. It took the burden off the human back and put it on a wheel. It brought into being the wagon. First imagination created something. Then the reality developed.

The automobile, airplane, radio, and television all developed during my lifetime—these were all born in the imagination. The imagination is the mother of invention. It is the dream of the imagination before it comes into the hard reality of metal and stone.

Imagination occurs almost totally in the world of the unknown. Youth seems to believe that everything good has already been done, that most inventions have been developed. In the Silicon Valley in San Jose, California, they do not feel that way. In the world of electronics they believe anything they give you today will be out-of-date tomorrow. They work day and night making it that way.

We live in a whole world of glory and wonder far beyond what is known today. Let us use our imaginations! Human destiny will be influenced by imagination.

Meditation and Imagination

Meditation is one of the greatest sources of bringing imagination into being.

There is a lot of imagination near a jet-powered 747 at its takeoff. You see over two hundred tons gliding down the runway and then it goes up! You say, "How did that much metal, and those six hundred suitcases ever get into the air?" Imagination! Men saw it before it could be done.

There is not much imagination in a group of people talking, laughing, and jesting. That is where imagination lies dead.

David said, *"I...meditate in thy word"* (Psalm 119:48). He was talking to God. This creates spiritual images such as "I can run through a troop." He was speaking of armed soldiers. "I can jump over a wall," meaning that if the enemy put up a barrier, he would go over the top of it.

David, through imagination, slew a giant. He slew a bear. He slew a lion with his naked hands. Before David slew that giant, he had already seen it. You might think that imagination is a little wild. It is supposed to be.

If a person does not have imagination, he will not advance. There are people who live the same way all their lives. That is not God's way. Imagination creates bigger and better things every day! Imagination is never satisfied! Imagination is always hungry! Imagination is always reaching out! God wants you to have creative imagination.

Creative Imagination

In 2 Corinthians 11:3, the apostle Paul said to the church in Corinth through the power of the Holy Spirit,

"But I fear, lest by any means, as the serpent beguiled Eve through his subtlety, so your minds should be corrupted from the simplicity that is in Christ."

Paul was talking straight to their imaginations. The devil who deceived Eve would also corrupt their imagining powers—their minds. Paul was dealing with things like adultery, lying, murder, and robbery. He said not to let your creative imagination go in the wrong direction. The serpent beguiled Eve through his subtlety, deceiving her mind, so that her mind would be corrupted from the innocence that God intended.

The Four Elements of the Mind

Your mind has at least four primary elements.

1. Thought—you create, or make things.

2. Learning—training. Keep doing the same thing until you can do it easily.

3. Understanding—an area of education and comprehension. Some people have facts but do not understand them.

4. Imagination—the capacity to form mental pictures.

These are all wrapped up in the human brain. The human brain has thought, where you can create. The brain has learning potential. A mother can cook because she cooks every day. The father may not be able to cook at all; he may know only his own daily work. Learning is a training process—a process of knowing how to do certain things. Understanding means that you have comprehension of the thing, not only knowledge that it exists.

Today, man's imagination is under demonic attack. Satan would like to destroy man's imagination, especially in the direction of God.

25
Passive Imagination

◆◆◆

In this chapter we will explore passive imagination. Second Corinthians 10:5 says, *"Casting down imaginations."* That means you have the power and authority to do whatever you want to with your imagination. You are not circumscribed to being a victim of imagination. It says, *"Casting down imaginations, and every high thing that exalteth itself against the knowledge of God."*

Anything that brings itself against God should be cast down, *"bringing into captivity every thought to the obedience of Christ."* This is one of the greatest verses in the whole Bible. If you are going to imagine evil or passive things, your imagination will never be positive. It will never be creative.

When you walk in the Spirit, you do not fulfill the lusts of the flesh. Rather than leaving your mind idle, put something constructive in there. With passive imagination you do not have to face the real issues of life, but you dream about things beyond reality.

Mental Depression

Passive imagination can bring you to a state of mental depression. You realize you are not getting anywhere, and you are sad about it.

Finally, or ultimately, a passive imagination could result in suicide. The devil says to your mind, "You are not wanted; nobody cares for you. You are worthless."

This is Satan's lie. Maybe many people love you. The truth is that your imagination is manipulated by the devil. That is why God says to cast down imaginations and anything that exalts itself against knowledge, reality, and truth. Anything that is not relative to truth ought to be cast down. You should not permit it to exist in any form whatsoever.

Imagination and Fear

Sometimes fear injects itself into imagination. Job, one of the famous men of the Bible, said in Job 3:25, *"For the thing which I greatly feared is come upon me, and that which I was afraid of is come unto me."*

Job's mind functioned with imagination. It conjured up a picture of desolation. Job had no apparent reason for believing that dark things or evil times lay ahead of him, but he imagined that they would come.

A man once said, "I've got enough meat in my house for this winter. I have enough young hogs for next winter. I have enough sows to bear pigs enough for the following winter, but what am I going to do the winter thereafter?"

The devil would like for you to have stupid thinking like that. What am I going to do when I get old? You will enjoy what you have made when you were young, of course. If you wasted it, then you are a waster, and the government will have to take care of you. You must prepare for the future. You should start preparing for the future the day you are born, and you keep preparing for it. There are people forty and fifty years old who wasted their lives, thinking they would never have any future. Then they turn sixty-five years old and say, "I have wasted my money, I have wasted my life, I have hated my friends, I abused my family, and now I am alone." You were alone all the time. If you imagine right, correct, holy, and good things, you will have a good ending to your life.

Fear originates in the mind—not just the brain.

God desires the human mind to be under divine subjection—not making up something that is not real. God does not want you to say, "I have plenty now, but I am afraid for tomorrow." There are millionaires who believe they are going to have to beg for bread before they die!

God demands that man's mind be directed by spiritual and not his soulical parts. This is very important. The agency of the Holy Spirit works with the human spirit.

Above all, the devil wants to capture the human mind and every aspect of it, including its imagination. The mind is so important, it becomes a battlefield. The devil wants your mind and God wants it. Your decision makes the difference.

Imagination and Blindness

Imagination can be related to blindness. Second Corinthians 4:4 says, *"In whom the god of this world hath blinded the minds of them which believe not."* If your mind is blinded, then your imagination is blinded. A blind mind cannot see itself as great or successful. If your mind is blinded, you cannot see deliverance. The Bible says the god of the world—the devil—has blinded your mind and imagination, lest the light of the glorious Gospel of Christ should shine unto them. God can increase your powers of imagination, and bring illumination so you can imagine great, new, and better things for your future.

Romans 1:28 says that all the heathen in the world become so by imagination. *"And even as they did not like to retain God in their knowledge, God gave them over to a reprobate mind* [a mind that could not think straight], *to do those things which are not convenient."*

The sinner is in an imaginative state that does not produce joy, happiness, or goodness. It produces pain, hurt, sorrow, and death. Your imagination can be blinded by sin, the devil, and evil, so that you cannot imagine good things. God does not want you to have such a life.

Imagination and Impression

We are primarily creatures of thought. Without thought the human is nothing. Your mind is your organ of thought. With your mind you know, think, imagine, and understand. These are the functions of the mind. Man's mind has power to reason, decide, and imagine unborn things. He has the power to bring them into being. The human mind occupies a large part of the total life of the human person. It determines the actions that he performs. That is the reason we call imagination the hidden force of human destiny.

Your mind is impressive. The mind of man has always been a place of challenge. What are you going to imagine? What are you going to be?

In Noah's day, the people imagined evil. After Noah's day, they imagined that God would again flood the earth, even after He had promised He would never do it. Man, in his imagination against God, built the Tower of Babel as his security.

God desires man's mind to function by the power of his spirit. Otherwise, he is unregenerate. The unregenerate man does not function by his spirit. If he has one, it does not function. Satan wants you to think about adultery and not marriage. He wants you to always think about what will destroy you. He makes you think, "Oh, that's fun." Just go to the hospitals and talk to the people with AIDS. See how much fun sin is. Go to the prostitute in jail and ask her how much fun sin is. Proverbs 14:34 says, *"Sin is a reproach to any people."*

Paul said this to the church of Ephesus:

Among whom also we all had our conversation in times past in the lusts of our flesh, fulfilling the desires of the flesh and of the mind; and were by nature the children of wrath, even as others. (Ephesians 2:3)

In Ephesians 4:22–23, Paul continued,

That ye put off concerning the former conversation the old man, which is corrupt according to the deceitful lusts; and be renewed in the spirit of your mind.

Your imagination comes out of your mind. God says He can renew those things, make them all over again. He can change their color, take off the old paint and put on new. He can make it all new on the inside. You do not have to live with passive imaginations.

In Colossians 1:21, Paul further said, *"And you, that were sometime alienated and enemies in your mind by wicked works, yet now hath he reconciled."*

At one time they were enemies of God in their minds. It was changed by the power of God. Romans 8:7 says, *"Because the carnal mind is enmity against God."*

If any person incorporates evil into his imagination, God says such a mind becomes an enemy to God.

Passive Imagination Is Empty

If your mind is empty, the devil will activate it. If you do not know what to think about, the devil will give you something. Passive imagination means that you have an imagination waiting for a power to activate it. It requires having a mind. The danger of ESP practitioners and gurus is that they tell you to put your mind in neutral. A blank mind is a great danger, because the devil can put any evil in it.

Your imagination must never go blank! It must forever be bringing in new things, new beauties and new wonders. A Christian must exercise his imaginative power.

Imagination and Inactivity

Imaginative inactivity is when you cease to use your full measure of creativity. During your older years your mind will grow stronger than it was in your younger years. Your powers of imagination should be stronger at the end of your life than at the beginning of your life.

God never desires inertia, whether you are young or old. When the mind ceases to create and comprehend, then the mind is actually sick. Your mental process should never be under bondage of any kind. The inactive mind needs to do things; it desires to do things, but it never does them.

Paul was strong in his instruction to the Ephesians who needed direction, just as we do today. Ephesians 4:17 says, *"This I say therefore, and testify in the Lord, that ye henceforth walk not as other Gentiles walk, in the vanity of their mind."*

Your powers of imagination must be used to imagine new things. Before you can have a new church building, you have to imagine it. You have to see it in the power of your imagination. Before you can have a great crowd of people, you must see them with the power of your spiritual imagination.

In Colossians 2:18, the same great apostle said,

> *Let no man beguile you of your reward in a voluntary humility and worshipping of angels, intruding into those things which he hath not seen, vainly puffed up by his fleshly mind.*

We have been warned time and again that the imagination cannot run loose; it must be harnessed. Otherwise, you will be vainly puffed up in a fleshly mind, displeasing to God, and not a blessing to yourself.

Paul had an unusual insight into imagination. In Titus 1:15 he said, *"Unto the pure all things are pure: but unto them that are defiled and unbelieving is nothing pure; but even their mind and conscience is defiled."* If a person has a wrong imagination, everything is ugly. To these people nothing is pure.

Your imagination can go against God in the area of worry. Worry is a type of inactivity. You just do not take the time to work; you just worry. The mind becomes weakened to the point where it cannot function, because all you do is worry. What we need in our power of imagination is concentration. The devil will interfere with anyone's concentration, especially a Christian's concentration. He does not want people to have the power of direction in their mental abilities.

Some people are totally powerless to concentrate. For your imagination to be great, you must have the power of concentration.

In other people, their power of concentration is flighty. To keep a person's attention over five minutes is a big job—television and other mass media cause the mind to go quickly from one thing to another, until human concentration is flighty. You can never be a great person until your imagination gets into an area of concentration where you can direct it toward God.

Another situation to consider is vacillation. The devil likes us to take opposite views of the same thing. The devil would like for us to generate one kind of thought and then immediately shift it to another kind of thought. Shifting shows the work of the adversary within us. Vacillation of the mind is the devil's tool. If you are going to vacillate between right and wrong, good and bad, then you will not ever get anything done. In order for your powers of imagination to operate, vacillation must go.

26
Imagination of the Ungodly

◆●◆

*W*e have studied imagination from several aspects—the birth of human imagination, creative imagination, and passive imagination. Another essential aspect is the imagination of the ungodly.

Adam's power of imagination was one of the most tremendous faculties he had when God created him. His power of imagination was divine.

God has imagination. The mighty galaxies in the heavens reveal the imagination of God. He created these mighty dimensions of glory and light.

Jesus said He was going to build mansions for His people. That is imagination!

Before Adam rebelled against God and his faculties were tarnished by sin, he possessed resplendent forces of imagination. For example, in his amazing reserve of imaginative powers, Adam had the ability to name every creature on the earth. One little creature grunted and he said, "You're a pig." Another little creature growled, and he said, "You're a dog." Another little creature meowed, and he said, "You're a cat." What an imagination! Adam named all the creatures of the earth and even remembered their names. No one else has been able to remember all their names!

However, in Adam's fallen state he became rebellious against the Creator who made him. His perfection of godliness was tarnished, and he became another person because of his corruption.

It is possible that only God has the innate ability to fully understand the mighty power of imagination. Modern science and psychology seek to understand it. However, God has said from the beginning that in Him imagination was good, and without Him it was bad.

Genesis 8:21 says, *"And the LORD smelled a sweet savour; and the LORD said in his heart, I will not again curse the ground any more for man's sake; for the imagination of man's heart is evil from his youth."* Children think evil and conceive evil things.

If natural man's power of choice is not yielded to the divine, holy, and pure, it is yielded to evil. This condition is prevalent in the world today. Sinners indulge in the world of fantasy—imagination. Some believe it to be a hidden world of self-enjoyment, which is not true. God's Word says in Mark 4:22 that every thought and intent of the heart will be made manifest and judged. There is nothing hidden.

Some people believe that ungodly and impure imaginations are wrong only when they become an act. If they hate a person and want to kill him, but do not do it, it is all right. However, you will be judged by what is on the inside of your heart, even though it has not been revealed or acted upon.

The imaginary processes are moving now. If you do not turn them into a godly, truthful, holy perception, they will naturally go according to the Adamic nature that is in rebellion against God.

The universal truth is that sinful man demonstrates what he imagines in his mind and God will judge him for it.

How did all this ungodly imagination start when man was once clean? God could have made man a zombie or an animal without imaginative powers. God created man to be an immortal and reproductive creature who could produce another generation of persons like himself. In that creation you discover the powers of imagination.

How did man fall from this lofty and high perception of God through holy imaginations to a low, evil imagination? You have heard the cliché "the devil made me do it." Well, I do not know about other times, but he did it this time.

It was Lucifer's imagination that led him to a state of revolt in heaven. It caused him to turn against and refrain from following God. Lucifer, the devil, began to see himself exalted—that's imagination!

The prophet Isaiah gave us an insight into Lucifer's self-exaltation. In Isaiah 14:13, the Holy Spirit revealed that the archangel Lucifer said in heaven, *"I will exalt my throne above the stars of God."* This means that he had power and authority in some places, but not at the throne of God. At the throne he was a servant. His goal was to exalt his throne above others. That self-exaltation is the power of imagination.

The devil determined he was not satisfied with his position even though he was great and beautiful.

Arrogantly, Satan said, *"I will exalt my throne above the stars of God."* He not only willed to ascend into heaven, but also sought to exalt his throne above the stars of God. This means there are thrones in heaven, places of strength and power.

Why did God give the archangel Lucifer such power? You cannot have a free moral agent without the power of choice. Intelligent people are either mentally competent or zombies. You possess the power of loving and following God or the power to rebel and not follow Him. If you did not have a choice, you would be a slave. God does not want slaves.

Vain Imagination Is a Yoke

Today, this imagination of rebellion, promoted by the devil, is a yoke of bondage to humans. Evil imagination is a yoke, a burden, and a sorrow.

> *And it shall come to pass in that day, that his burden shall be taken away from off thy shoulder, and his yoke from off thy neck, and the yoke shall be destroyed because of the anointing.*　　　　(Isaiah 10:27)

God will use the power of the Holy Spirit to destroy the vain imaginations of the devil. He will deliver us from all evil thinking, anything, everything—God will set us free by His mighty power!

The Bible states that evil imagination is not something nice, easy, or good.

Evil imaginations are a hindrance to a successful life. God says to you, "I can break the yoke, and the yoke shall be destroyed by My holy anointing." God breaks the yoke of ungodly imaginations and sets you free by His mighty power. Receive it and walk in it!

Some church leaders talk to me about problems with morals, fear, and finances. They get discouraged and want to quit. I assure them that God can destroy the yoke.

God can destroy your yoke. He can destroy the power of evil imaginations and bring you into a place of deliverance! God says the yoke will be destroyed by the holy anointing. God is ready right now to cause your imaginations to be pure, clean, and holy unto Himself.

King Solomon spoke these words regarding imagination in Proverbs 6:18, *"An heart that deviseth wicked imaginations, feet that be swift in running to mischief."*

Ungodly imaginations will cause you to do evil and run, not just walk, to it.

The imaginations of the righteous are righteousness—they run the other direction.

The ungodly devise wicked imaginations or fantasies of evil. There are millions of men and women who fantasize evil and immorality. Solomon said these imaginations come up out of the heart, which is the emotional center of the human personality.

In Proverbs 23:7, *"For as he thinketh in his heart, so is he."* Your imaginations are what you think. If you think evil, you are evil. If you think good, then you will certainly be good.

Imagination and Lust

I am sure that lust is an imagination. It is an image of human fantasy. Lust terminates in the sins of moral and spiritual death. Lust will destroy any human who fantasizes with it. The imaginations of the lustful lead to spiritual poverty. They lead to destruction. They lead to hell. God wants us to be free from strange lusts. I urge you in the name of Jesus to keep yourself free from them.

Imagination and Hate

The imaginations of hate are self-destroying. Hate imagines and visualizes how to get even with people and destroy them. These come from Satan, not from God. Hate imagines revenge. Hate is a cancer of your imagination, mind, emotions, and will. It is a destroyer.

Do not let your imaginations be full of hate, desiring to get revenge and wanting to hurt another person.

Imaginations causing anger and stirring up your passions are destructive. Many say they have been mistreated, so they retaliate. Do not let anger cause cancer of the spirit and soul. It will destroy the peace of the inner man. Hate is a monster. Get rid of it as quickly as you can, in Jesus' name.

Imagination and Sorrow

A further imagination is sorrow. Psychologists and psychiatrists tell us that if you are still mourning ninety days after a tragedy, it is self-interest and self-pity. You are feeling sorry for yourself.

It is so easy to permit your imagination to overwhelm you in sorrow. Your imagination fantasizes on how bad things are and how sad you are. You have reasons to be sad, and you ought to be sad. You believe earth is a world of sorrow.

I must tell you sorrow will destroy you. In Romans 14:17 we read, *"For the kingdom of God is not meat and drink; but righteousness, and peace, and joy in the Holy Ghost."*

Whatever happens, we must live in the kingdom of peace and of joy, as God wants us to live. Please rise above the abyss of sorrow!

Imagination and Failure

You know that it is not what happens to you that counts; it is how you react to what happens to you that counts.

If your self-image is marked with hopelessness, then it originates in your powers of imagination. You must imagine success, victory, and fulfillment.

When you are a believer, you are not a failure. Then do not imagine failure!

Of tremendous value is the fact that you can imagine an untruth. The situation is not true; you have imagined it. You can fantasize that someone does not like you, when in fact, he really does like you. You have not opened your heart to truth. An impaired imagination can lead you to believe untruth.

Your imagination can seek out a friend or relative and say this one did not like me and that one did not like me. Maybe they do! Even if they do not care for you, it is possible to teach them to like you by being nice to them.

Chambers of Imagery

Ezekiel 8:12 says,

Then said he unto me, Son of man, hast thou seen what the ancients of the house of Israel do in the dark, every man in the chambers of his imagery? for they say, The LORD seeth us not; the LORD hath forsaken the earth.

God said His people had chambers of imagery on the inside. In these chambers they teach that *"the LORD seeth us not."* They continue, *"the LORD hath forsaken the earth."* What fatalism!

God wants you to know that there are no secret places He cannot look into. There are no conditions He cannot understand.

I was in a missionary's home in South America. We were sitting in the living room talking and his little son came walking in. The lad looked to be about five or six years old. He said, "Daddy, can Jesus see?" The father replied, "Yes, He can." Then we looked at the boy and he said, "Daddy, can Jesus see under our house?" The missionary said, "Yes, Jesus can see under our house." The son shook his head sadly and said, "I sure wish Jesus was blind."

I said to the father, "You had better have a look under the house!"

God wants us to know that He knows our hearts; He knows our thinking. God loves us!

God can erase everything the devil has done and start you over from today with the right kind of imagery in your heart.

Empty Imaginations

The apostle Paul said it this way in Romans 1:21, *"Because that, when they knew God, they glorified him not as God, neither were thankful; but became vain [empty] in their imaginations, and their foolish heart was darkened."*

They became empty in their imaginations. A lot of imaginations are scatterbrained or nothing but foolishness. God can cause your imaginations to be strong, alive, and pleasing to Him. You hold the reins. Do not blame it on someone else. Do not say the devil talked in your ear. He is not on the inside if he is outside talking. You command him, "Go," and he has to go!

I urge you not to let the devil conquer you in your imaginations and cause them to be empty and unfruitful. They can be fruitful in creating the beautiful things of life.

By the way of personal testimony, I would not have the beautiful home and family I have today if I had not seen it when I was young. When I got married I knew what I wanted. With our three sons, Louise and I knew what we wanted. Today with our ten grandchildren we know what we want. Our imaginations have come to beautiful fruition on the domestic level and the spiritual level.

I have been growing and maturing as of this moment in God. That is what I want you to do. I want your imaginations to be pure, holy, and energized by the power of the Holy Spirit!

27
The Human Mind and Spiritual Health

◆●◆

The spirit can be only as healthy as the human mind. First Corinthians 2:16 says that we have the mind of Christ. What is the mind of Christ? If you have the mind of Christ, you have a strong mind. You have a mind that never knows fear. You have a mind that cannot be defeated. You have a mind that knows what is going to happen tomorrow. If we have the mind of Christ, we have a victorious mind. The greatest battle that you will ever face on this earth will be in the area of your mind.

The passive mind has no power of concentration. The passive mind finds it impossible to concentrate. When the devil interferes with the power of mental concentration, some people become totally powerless in their concentration. They cannot memorize anything. Others concentrate in a flighty way. They can think of a thing for a moment or two, and then their mind is off on something else. We can learn to develop powers of concentration so that we can stay on one thing as long as necessary. We should discipline ourselves to concentrate.

The passive mind has to do with forgetfulness. There are some people who are deprived of a powerful memory. They forget what they just said or did. They cannot locate an article that they had in their hands five minutes earlier. Natural loss of memory is an attack of the devil trying to cause us to lose our self-confidence. It damages our usefulness.

The Devil Wants to Destroy You

One of the ways the devil has of destroying you is through your mind. When we accept passivity as an attack of Satan, then we know how to fight it. We know how to resist and come against it.

One of the symptoms of a passive mind is vacillation. The devil will take a person's mind and cause him to take opposite views very quickly. This is very dangerous. You must know what you believe and live according to the moral nature within you. You must be on one side or the other. If you take opposite sides on a subject very quickly, then you have a problem with your mind. The devil makes us generate one kind of thought and immediately shifts us to another kind of thought. That shifting admits the work of the adversary in our lives. A vacillating mind is the devil's tool. The Word of God tells us that an unstable mind is like the sea. God wants us to make a decision and stick with it. If you know something, know it! If you believe something, believe it!

The unrelaxed mind is very dangerous. Insomnia is common in our country. It is the work of the enemy. People will lie in bed for endless hours thinking of all sorts of things. They count sheep and everything else, but their minds are like machines that will not turn off. Sometimes a car will keep idling after the engine is turned off. Some people's minds are like that. They lie down and turn their minds off, but they just keep chugging. This is from the devil. The Bible says the Lord gives His beloved sleep. There is only one thing that can happen to an unrelaxed mind: it will break. Many people in insane asylums today are there because of unrelaxed minds. We should have power over our minds and say, "All right. You can relax now," and it will relax right there.

Many people commit suicide because they are unable to relax inside. They are all keyed up and cannot stop. They just go until the devil destroys them. In the twenty-third psalm, David said that there is a place of tranquility and peace in God, whatever happens to you. You can say to your mind, "Go to sleep now," and the mind has to calm down. You can command it to do so. If you cannot make your mind obey you, then it is rebellious. You never know what a rebel is going to do. Anytime you want to go to first base, he may take off for third, and you will have problems and sorrows. You must control your mind.

Many people let their minds wander. Their minds run around and do anything they please. They have not disciplined their minds to think the things they should think and do the things they should do. Your mind must obey because you make it obey.

If your brain starts playing games with you, talk to it. "Hey, brain, I have some news for you. I'm going to cause you to think right. Why don't you read Romans 8:1, *'There is therefore now no condemnation to them which are in Christ Jesus.'*" Disobedient minds have done a lot of damage to human beings. Maybe they had no one to help them, to pray with them, or teach them to relax. I am a relaxed person. I am not keyed up, and I do not ever intend to be tense.

Let Jesus Rule Your Life

My whole life is governed by Jesus. The things I do such as teaching, preaching, television work, and writing books are all just part of my work for God. They all have to move together in the will and purpose of God. I will not permit any single thing to become a dictator over my life. I learned how to pray years ago. When I knelt down, the devil began telling me the things I needed to do. I could not get my mind to concentrate on praying because of all these flashing thoughts. I said, "I'll take care of you." As I knelt down to pray, I put my writing pad beside me. Then I said, "Now, just give them to me, and I'll write them down for you." When the devil saw that I was getting serious about praying and controlling my thoughts, he left. Sometimes there would not be anything on the pad.

You have to become the king of your mind. Flashing thoughts must not dominate and disturb you. Where there is a multitude of words there is no lack of sin. If the devil can get you to constantly talk, then you never listen. You will not learn much. There are some people who can be in the audience of a great man who may be saying something very important, but they are not hearing a thing he is saying. They are just waiting for him to pause so they can jump in and say something silly. The great thoughts of the teacher just drift through their minds like the wind, and they are all gone. Many people just talk and gossip and backbite and joke. A torrent of words runs through their brains and mouths, but nothing remains.

What happens to the subconscious or subliminal mind at night? Is there any hope of working on our minds during our sleep? I want to believe there is. I believe that when we pray before we go to bed we can take command of our minds. We can say to the devil, "You can't get in here tonight. No nightmares! If I have dreams, they're going to be sweet ones." Some dreams are inspired by God, but others are certainly generated by the devil. While some dreams produce psychic conditions, others form part of the mental pictures that developed during the day. They come back to you in the evening. During sleep the brain is less active, and its passive spirit can be manipulated. Sometimes the manipulation is by the devil. Some dreams cause people to wake up despondent. Sleep did not replenish their strength. They say, "I got up feeling tired and miserable. I did not have any rest."

When you lie down to sleep, you must take command of your mind. We can cause ourselves to have sweet dreams of spiritual things. Nine out of ten dreams that I have, I am preaching and souls are saved by the hundreds and thousands. I awake refreshed! I believe one reason is that I have commanded my mind to refresh itself even while I sleep. I command it to slow down and bring inspiring thoughts to my total man.

Romans 10:5 says, *"For Moses describeth the righteousness which is of the law, that the man which doeth those things shall live by them."* God wants us to live by certain principles. If you live that way, your mind will be that way.

Ephesians 4:17–18 teaches,

This I say therefore, and testify in the Lord, that ye henceforth walk not as other Gentiles walk, in the vanity of their mind, having the understanding darkened, being alienated from the life of God through the ignorance that is in them, because of the blindness of their heart.

We do not have to live with our understanding darkened and alienated from the life of God through ignorance. God does not want us to be in such a condition. At salvation, man's mind undergoes a change. That is when you start working on your mind, saying, "Now my mind is unshackled and is going to become empowered. It is going to become exceedingly active and have an amazing power of concentration." Paul essentially said in 1 Corinthians 2:16, "I shall have, I will have, I must have the mind of Christ." I will have the mind of Christ.

The mind can have the same spiritual health as your body. When I see a person's mind sick or disturbed, I am upset inside. You can pray for a man's mental condition as well as for his fingers or any other part of his body. God can touch his mind as easily as He can touch any other part of the body. We shy away from that, but we must not be afraid of it. God wants our minds to become strong and powerful, but more than that He wants them to become spiritual. He wants our minds to be the incubators of spiritual life flowing out to others. Our minds should be full of good, precious, and wonderful things. God is able to make it so if we will yield our minds to Him and His spiritual truth. Anytime you close your mind to a thing, you blind it. There are millions of people who turn their minds away from spiritual truth. Your mind needs to be open and flowing. God is able to refurbish our minds every day. He is willing to both bless and strengthen our minds.

28
Spiritual Imagination

◆●◆
___

I never imagined I would ever teach on spiritual imagination. God awoke me from a sound sleep and poured into my spirit the force, power, and reality of imagination. God showed me it is the hidden force of human potential.

In 1 Corinthians 2:9 it says, *"But as it is written, Eye hath not seen, nor ear heard, neither have entered into the heart of man, the things which God hath prepared for them that love him."*

It is your imagination that will bring out and understand the magnificent things God has prepared for those who serve Him faithfully on the face of this earth.

You can involve yourself in spiritual imagination. God created man to imagine good things. Imagination is a spiritual and divine gift from the Most High God.

Not everyone is a Michaelangelo or Raphael. There are degrees of imagination. Whatever amount God has given you, use it. It is possible that no two people in history have had the same amount of imagination. It is a shame not to use what you have. It is possible that the greatest sources of imagination never come to fruition because they were not brought into the realm of reality.

The spiritual imagination can do many things for you. For example, if you are sick, you must see yourself well. The source of this imagination is faith in God and the Bible. If you are depressed, you must see your depression gone. There is spiritual and physical healing in the area of your human spirit. You first see it on the inside, and then one day you realize it on the outside.

There are spiritual dimensions in imagination that have never been fathomed. Many people have not been taught the greatness of imagination. God wants us to understand the faculties that He has given us in order to grow spiritually. One of the greatest is imagination.

The devil surely knows this. He hates imagination, and he puts his counterfeits in the human mind. Alcoholic beverages are an example. An alcoholic beverage is taken in order to hallucinate. That and other drugs create images and mental suggestions that are not normal or natural. It is the power of imagination, but it will destroy your future.

Isaiah 28:7 says,

> *But they also have erred through wine, and through strong drink are out of the way; the priest and the prophet have erred through strong drink, they are swallowed up of wine, they are out of the way through strong drink; they err in vision, they stumble in judgment.*

Drinking alcoholic beverages is not the right way to live. The reason you drink wine and liquor is to get a new high. The men and women who drink alcohol often have automobile accidents, lose their jobs, children, homes, spouses, and finally their souls. Alcohol is only the devil's counterfeit for imagination. You must not follow the devil's counterfeit. You must follow the righteousness of God who created you with imagination. God made it. He put it there for you to use for good things.

The power of drugs and alcohol brings you into a netherworld—or underworld—of hideous creatures. That is what is called delirium tremens. A person suffering from delirium tremens sees demons all around, running at him, piercing him, poking him, grinning at him. His imagination fell to the bottom by using the devil's counterfeit of what God wants to do. The devil is the biggest counterfeiter the world ever knew. Do not follow the devil's counterfeit!

How strong is the power of imagination? David desired to be king of Israel. He used the power of imagination to accomplish this. A new nation was born when he stepped into office. He consolidated unrelated tribes, some living miles apart, into a central government in Jerusalem. He further consolidated them with a religious power in Jerusalem. This unity had to be in his brain first. No one can build a nation thoughtlessly or by accident. David understood the power of spiritual imagination. He directed it into fulfillment. David had success because he first imagined and then achieved it.

Many people ask, "How can you keep imagination running in the right avenue where it is constructive? Who is the builder?" The Holy Spirit speaks to us in 1 Peter 1:13, *"Wherefore gird up the loins of your mind."* Your loins are the strength you pull with. If you are pulling a heavy load, you lower your head and let your loins do the pulling.

The human mind has pulling power. When you gird it up, it is like putting a harness on your mind. This harness guides and controls it.

The apostle said, *"Be sober"* (v. 13). He was not talking about alcoholic beverages, but about excessive nonsense. Your imagination can get into stupidity and silliness. Peter said to be sober and have hope. Hope is an area of imagination.

You can bring hope into focus, push it with faith, and your imagination will become reality. The apostle Paul said in 1 Corinthians 2:16, *"For who hath known the mind of the Lord, that he may instruct him? But we have the mind of Christ."* Now move that thought into imagination. We have the imagination of Christ. Christ wanted to save the world. We, as His disciples, have the same imagination inside us. Christ desires that all who are sick would be healed. We have that imagination inside us. We want to go to heaven. Christ is already there preparing a place for us, and we imagine ourselves there.

It is easy for me to say that when you are born again, salvation harnesses your imagination, but it would not be honest or true.

Remember, there is bitterness in the heart of the devil because he lost heaven. There is a hatred in his heart because God disciplined and judged him. The devil will come against anyone God loves, and you are the apex of His love. The strongest force you have is your mind, so Satan comes against your mind. He will seek to enter your world of imagination and cause you to imagine wrong, unspiritual, and evil things, rather than permit your imagination to be what God ordained it to be: spiritual, clean, and holy.

You resist Satan by directing your spirit through the Holy Spirit. Your imagination should flow from your spirit into your mind. Your spirit will let you know whether your imagination is of God or not. When Christians filter their remarkable imaginations through their born-again experience with God, their soulical parts become integrated into their spiritual parts. Their Adamic natures become part of their spiritual nature. That is when God can do His best. That is when we create more than at any other time. That is when God can do something really good and great for you.

There is a spiritual battle. God knows it, and you will find it out soon. The battle should be directed through your spirit. You can fight the devil in the spirit when you cannot fight him any other way. When Satan wants to capture your mind, move in the Spirit; then he is defeated and destroyed by God's power.

God foresees all imagination in its embryo stage, not just in the fullness of its power.

How much Christian authority do we have in the realm of imagination? In 2 Corinthians 10:5 these words are written, *"Casting down imaginations, and every high thing that exalteth itself against the knowledge of God."* If the devil puts a false imagination in your mind, knock it down. The Bible says to cast down every imagination that is not of God and bring into captivity every thought to the obedience of Christ. Now that is authority! God leaves the responsibility to you, not to Him. He tells *you* to cast down imaginations. He has already saved you. He has already given you the power. He has already given you the authority. God shouts, "You cast it down!"

The Bible says that the devil is a liar and you cannot accept his imaginations. The devil exalts himself against the knowledge of God.

Our powers of thought are subservient and obedient to God, if we bring them into captivity. It is great for every thought to be obedient to Christ. The human mind possesses unlimited activity, ability, and authority! The powers of imagination have never been fathomed on the face of this earth. The Christian has the authority to cast down any unholy imagination. God has called us to holiness in our thought life. We are what we imagine ourselves to be. If you are going to imagine yourself as a devastated failure, the devil will help you become one.

The word *image* comes from "imagination," or "imagery." God wants you to imagine prosperity, health, and all the blessings that belong to you. God wants you to enjoy and move into them. They belong to you!

When you are born again, God changes your total destiny—mind, thought life, creative life, and power of imagination—the total complex area of mental power. Christ changes your emotional power and willpower. When we are born again, we must bring our imaginations to God where they belong.

If we could get Christian imagination running high in this country, we could change the whole world. We need to imagine how to save the whole world. We need to imagine how to bring greater produce into the world. We have men working now on saving the world from starvation. I have a friend in California whose life is obsessed with learning how to feed the millions who are starving today. Let your imagination rise up! This is the moment for powerful imagination to be born in our hearts, to realize the horizons are our limits, and that we are reaching to the stars to do great things for God!

Let God bless your imagination with strength and power. Place your imagination under the guidance of the Holy Spirit; then you will not imagine wrong things.

Do you realize the power of your own personal imagination? Do you see how you can make it work in your own spiritual growth?

Your imagination can create health and wealth. The devil wants to steal your spiritual imagination and push you into the abyss of moral filth.

We all need to become super-productive in our imagination. There are a thousand ways for every one of us to make a living. We do not need to be dependent on the government. Let your spirit rise up in holy imagination to be something great in God. Rise up in spiritual strength. Imagine yourself like Paul or Moses, a tremendous spiritual success. Do that in Jesus' name!

29
The Soul in Controversy with the Spirit

❧❧

The Bible teaches us that there is a battle between what Adam was and what Christ is. You have the key. You can live either life.

Romans 6:7–8 says, *"For he that is dead is freed from sin. Now if we be dead with Christ, we believe that we shall also live with him."* The only way to be free from sin is to die to it. Death does not only mean extinction. It can also mean separation. God said, "Separate yourself from this thing. Die to it!" If we are dead with Christ, we will also live with Him. Water baptism is symbolic of this truth. When you go down in the waters of baptism, you take your Adamic or carnal nature and submerge it into the waters. When it is covered by the waters, it is buried. When you come up out of the waters of baptism, your spirit is resurrected. That is the spirit life.

Paul said, "I die daily." That old nature will rise up again and again. You have to determine who will be the king of your life. If you are going to say, "I'm grieved; I'm sad," you are permitting your soulical parts to be the boss in your life. If you wake up and say, "Hallelujah! It's a new day! I'm looking for about a dozen Goliaths," you will see some giants fall down, and you will grow and increase spiritually. The spirit part of you will become great in your life.

Romans 7:22–23 says,

> *For I delight in the law of God after the inward man:*
> *but I see another law in my members, warring against*
> *the law of my mind, and bringing me into captivity to*
> *the law of sin which is in my members.*

Paul could see this controversy. If you study people you will see this controversy raging every day. Man's soul, especially in his unregenerate state, is in a state of rebellion against his spirit. This controversy between spirit and soul includes such things as resentment, self-pity, and self-defeat.

Don't Defeat Yourself

Did you know you can talk yourself out of every victory? You are not really defeated. You are self-defeated. This destruction comes from the wrong kind of a confession: "I cannot do anything today. I'm a failure. I cannot stand up to anyone." This is your soulical language. You can take that same tongue and say, "I am a victor! I win all the battles! I'm going through!" This is the spirit talking.

There is a controversy between your Adamic nature and your born-again nature. You must win the battle. God will not win it for you. I have seen some of the greatest people in the world feel inferior to others. There was no rhyme or reason for it. It was Satan causing them to think negatively. They were great. They had beautiful minds. They had beautiful personalities, but the devil said, "Oh, you're nothing. You can't do as well as others." These diabolical thoughts dominated their lives. This is a soulical matter, not spiritual at all. In Jesus Christ we are more than conquerors!

There are people who condemn themselves, saying, "I had a bad thought." You did not do it; the devil just put it in your ear. Tell him to get out of here and stay out!

There are millions of Christians walking around feeling condemned right now. It is a soulical problem. Romans 8:1 says, *"There is therefore now no condemnation to them which are in Christ Jesus, who walk not after the flesh, but after the Spirit."*

The human mind in its original state delights in the things of this world—things that are logical, or psychological. This is the realm of the soulish part. When we move in God, we move into another world of the Spirit. This is where God moves through our inner being and we know supernaturally what we should do. That is where God wants to live and be a victor in the controversy.

One of the classic examples of the controversy between soul and spirit in the whole Bible is Joseph. Genesis 45:3–8 says,

> *And Joseph said unto his brethren, I am Joseph; doth my father yet live? And his brethren could not answer him; for they were troubled at his presence. And Joseph said unto his brethren, Come near to me, I pray you. And they came near. And he said, I am Joseph your brother, whom ye sold into Egypt. Now therefore be not grieved, nor angry with yourselves, that ye sold me hither: for God did send me before you to preserve life. For these two years hath the famine been in the land: and yet there are five years, in the which there shall neither be earing nor harvest. And God sent me before you to preserve you a posterity in the earth, and to save your lives by a great deliverance. So now it was not you that sent me hither, but God: and he hath made me a father to Pharaoh, and lord of all his house, and a ruler throughout all the land of Egypt.*

The last time Joseph's brothers had seen him, they sold him for twenty pieces of silver. If your brothers sold you for twenty bucks and you became the governor of New York State and they came for some food, how would you treat them? The worst jailhouse would be the best place in town for them, wouldn't it?

The spirit of this man was strong and great. There is possibly no man in the Bible who excites me as much as Joseph does. He was mistreated most of his life. He spent seven years in jail for refusing to commit adultery. After coming out of prison at thirty years of age, he still had a sweet spirit inside him. That is what God wants of us. It does not matter how people treat you. Let your spirit prevail. Do not have self-pity. Do not moan about how you are mistreated and hurt. *Refuse to be hurt by people.*

There is a controversy in this world today. You will have to decide if you are going to let your spirit or your soul win.

30
The Spiritual Man

◆●◆

A medical doctor once told me that when he was saved and received the Holy Spirit, he changed 80 percent of his prescriptions. He said, "Before I was saved I learned certain methods in medical school. I gave advice and prescriptions according to what I learned. When God's Spirit entered me, I saw humans the way God sees them. I knew their needs, not from a medical sense, but from a spiritual sense. Many times I said, 'You know, you don't need any medicine. I'll pray for you. That's all you need.' I would pray for them, and they would go on their way."

Intuition Comes from God

Your spirit being is composed of several things.

Through your spirit you can know evil no one else knows about. You have intuition. You can meet someone and know more about him than he knows about himself. By looking at him, God speaks through your spirit about that person. You know good or evil just by coming into its presence. That intuition works in spiritual things. You begin to know God in a way that others do not know Him. To the sinner, God is the great big man upstairs. To you, He is not a man, and He is not upstairs. To you, He is right down inside you.

Intuition is one of the great propensities of the spirit-man within you. You must release it. You must let it flow and not inhibit it. God wants a free flow of the personality. All babies are born that way. When they come into the world, they are born with a free personality. When the spirit of man comes alive, a power of intuition begins to show you things other people do not see. We can know things in politics that others would not know. Christians have an advantage over everyone they meet, but you must talk slowly enough to let God speak through you.

You have a power called understanding. You understand people's feelings in a way that others do not understand. Other people might hurt someone, but you will not hurt him because you feel for him. You have intuition toward human life. The greatest place to release this is toward God. It gives you an insight into God. It gives you a revelation of God through the born-again spirit.

The next area of the spirit is communion. Your spirit, not your brain, is your center of communion. You may try to have mental communion with God, but you will not get very far. God does not respond to your brain. The Bible says, *"By wisdom* [men] *knew not God"* (1 Corinthians 1:21). You do not come to know God through earthly wisdom. You know God by faith and confession of your sins. Communion comes from the spirit part of you. Many people do not release this part of their spirit life. You can have communion with God anytime; He is there all the time. Communion goes further than God; it reaches out to man. Christians are the sweetest people in the world. They are the nicest folk on the face of this earth. God makes the difference.

Your Conscience

Another area of the spirit is conscience. Why can sinners do so many things that are bad and keep what we call a good conscience?

When I was in China, I studied the Chinese people all the time. As we were on the road going up to Tibet, I would ask them questions. I asked a man, "Is it wrong to steal?" I guess he had been guilty, because he looked around cautiously before answering me. I said, "Come on now, this is just between friends. Is it wrong to steal?" "Well," he finally responded, "I'll tell you. If no one finds it out, it's all right. But if someone finds out, it's really bad to steal." Then I backed up a little and retorted, "Now, you mean that doing it is not bad in itself?" He did not know what to say. "Well," his answer came, "you see, it is not embarrassing unless someone finds out." I said, "I'm not talking about embarrassment, I'm talking about God. You believe in a god, and you know good from bad." "Well," he rebuffed, "it is all right to do it if you don't get caught. That's all I know." I said, "No, that is not right. You should not do it if it is wrong. If it is bad, it is bad. It is never good if it is bad. You have to have a conscience in you." Part of your spirit is your conscience. Your conscience can grow.

Many years ago I was sitting down with a newspaper in my hand, reading the comics. A woman passed by and said, "Are you a Christian?" I replied, "Yes." She quipped, "It doesn't look like it." I cannot stand the comics to this day! No one, my wife or anyone else, has ever seen me read them. Why? My spirit came alive within me. The conscience part of me, said, "I'm bigger and better than that junk. I don't have to put that into my mind." Your conscience is different from other people's conscience. A born-again person has a different idea about life than anyone else through the conscience God has given him.

Sometimes people have what we call a seared conscience. It is burned out, worn out, and not used. Whatever was wrong when you first got saved is still wrong. I have heard people say, "You know when I first got saved I could not do this or that or the other thing, but I can do it all right now." That means they began in the Spirit and ended in the flesh. God wants us to live by our spirit. Your spirit is the king of your life! It must direct everything you do. The boss does not come from the emotions and thoughts of your soul. The authority comes from what God has planted on the inside of us through the Holy Spirit.

Put Christ on the Throne of Your Life

We must live, walk, pray, sing, and reign with Christ in the spirit. Then we become more than conquerors in the spirit. We have no condemnation, guilt, worry, or fear in our spirit. Our spirit will then take the royal nature upon itself.

He *"hath made us kings and priests unto God and his Father; to him be glory and dominion for ever and ever"* (Revelation 1:6). We have been made kings and priests in our spiritual parts, not in our soulical parts. We are not the same as a king on the throne of Europe. We are kings and priests in our spiritual realm. We rule spiritually.

The priest heals, and the king bosses. When your spirit becomes king of your life, a priestly nature flows through you to serve the whole personality. Then your spirit is the king of your life, your soul is the servant of your life, and your body is the slave of your life. If you do not keep them that way, you will never flow in the Spirit of God.

The Greek word *pneuma* means spirit, the human spirit. The Greek word *psuche* defines the human soul. Your human being is not naturally dirty. If it is bad, it is because the devil made it bad. The soul is not spiritual, but it is not dirty. It is what you make it as you grow.

Life Flows out of Our Bellies

We have within us a kingly spirit that rules the rest of our total personality. Your appetite cannot tell you how much to eat. Your spirit tells you how much to eat. If you do not function that way, you will be out of the Spirit of God. Proverbs 20:27 says, *"The spirit of man is the candle of the Lord, searching all the inward parts of the belly."* Christ said in John 7:38, *"Out of his belly shall flow rivers of living water."* That is how I discovered where a man's spirit is. God taught me that you have two thrones inside you. You have a throne over your souli-cal being centered in your mind, and a throne in your belly over your spiritual man.

"Out of his belly shall flow rivers of living water." Jesus has to be the king. The spirit-man has to be in charge. If your Adamic nature becomes the king, you will not live a victorious life. About 90 percent of the Christians I meet still live in their soulish nature. This is especially true in the area of intellect and emotions. If you are going to be controlled by your emotions, you will be like a little leaf on the water, constantly tossed back and forth.

31
What Is Conscience?

*H*omo sapiens is intriguingly designed, engineered, and perfected. After six thousand years of human study, man's innermost workings are still a mystery. Science may understand many things, but man is its greatest mystery.

Man witnesses and sees the beauty of the universe with two instruments called eyes. He feels with his total personality all the vibrations of human experience.

Man's inner mechanisms of mind and emotions spur the imagination, conscience, and memory beyond definition. You can struggle with them, but they baffle scientific minds.

The human conscience is one of the greatest gifts God gave to man. The Bible says in Acts 24:16, *"And herein do I exercise myself, to have always a conscience void of offence toward God, and toward men."*

What is the "voice of conscience"? What does it mean to have a conscience?

When we say, "Man has a conscience," what do we mean?

If a man drives a hard bargain with someone, his neighbors will say, "That fellow has no conscience." What is really lacking in that person?

Without a conscience man would be an animal. He would not be a human person. He would not be "made in the image and likeness of God." Man's conscience is part of his soulical part, not his spirit. It is part of our Adamic nature and not our born-again spirit nature.

The word *conscience* comes to us from a Latin word *conscire,* which means "con-science" or "with knowing." The word *conscientia* means "a moral sense of knowledge."

The word *conscience* comes from a Greek word *suneidesis,* which means "knowing or to know the truth." Conscience means knowing truth.

Conscience is the faculty by which we comprehend the will of God. It is a function and operation from the soulish part of us.

The conscience is designed to govern our lives. A sense of guilt before God comes through conscience. It helps us know how we should live before God. Hebrews 10:2 says, *"For then would they not have ceased to be offered? because that the worshippers once purged should have had no more conscience of sins."*

In the Old Testament, sin was forgiven at the time of sacrifice. When an Old Testament believer committed another sin, he had to return and ask for forgiveness again. God says the offerings that were offered at that time took away the conscience of sins. The Lord Jesus does not function in that way. He does not have to die every year, month, or day. Christ died one time. He purged our consciences. Mankind is still purged after two thousand years.

Conscience distinguishes what is considered morally good or bad. It commends us if we are good and condemns us if we are bad.

Conscience is the ability to evaluate, judge, and justify the works or thoughts you have.

Conscience cannot be measured. It is an explosive power that permeates your total being. It functions through all your soulical parts: your mind, feelings, and decisions.

Human conscience was not a part of man's nature until Adam and Eve ate the fruit of the Tree of the Knowledge of Good and Evil in the Garden of Eden. Kenneth Taylor wrote in his *Living Bible* that the tree Adam and Eve ate of was the "Tree of Conscience."

As a soulical power, conscience is neutral. The conscience can become spiritual through spiritual rebirth. Conscience can become evil if you lend yourself to evil. Then human conscience is no longer neutral.

The Bible says that some people's consciences are seared with a hot iron because of wrong decisions. They do what is wrong. Your conscience can be carnal or it can be spiritual. Man has to decide what kind of conscience he desires inside himself.

The apostle Paul said, "I want a conscience void of offense to God." Then he paused and said, "I want a conscience void of offense to man."

He had the capacity to choose whether his conscience would be a spiritual conscience or a sinful conscience. You have the authority within yourself to decide what kind of conscience you will have. You can make your conscience tenderer by drawing closer to God.

God does not tell anyone to live by his conscience. He tells us to live by the blood of Jesus Christ that cleanses us from our sins so that we can be holy before Him and live according to His Word.

When I traveled to Alaska, I enjoyed one of the most beautiful boat rides up the Inland Passage between Seattle and Juneau. One night as the boat made its way, I was walking on the top deck and found the captain. He was walking alone, so I got in step and walked with him.

It was a beautiful starry night as the two of us walked the top deck, back and forth. I leaned over and said, "Captain, who is Jesus? Whose son was He?" It was amazing how angry the captain became. He knew it was a religious question, and he let me know that he was not religious. I was almost sorry he was the captain.

The captain looked up and said, "Those stars are my gods. They have guided me for fifty years." I touched him on the arm and said, "Do you know that my God created your gods?"

How did the sea captain arrive at such a conclusion? His conscience was out of balance with the Word and Spirit of God. It was out of balance with reality. The man worshipped stars made of gases and minerals.

We use the word *conscience* in interesting ways. An example is the conscientious objector. He is a person who objects to military service on the grounds that his conscience forbids him to take up arms. In London, England, they have the Court of Conscience. It is used for the recovery of small debts, usually to keep petty grievances out of the big courts.

In Scotland the trams and buses have a small box in the back. That special box is there to put your fare in if the conductor is busy at the other end of the tram or bus and cannot get to you. It is called a Conscience Box. I was intrigued to watch people when they got off the tram. If the conductor had not gotten to them, they would put their threepence or sixpence in that box. When I spoke to the conductor about the box, he said, "The Conscience Box is full every day." Those people slept well at night.

Your conscience is like a compass. It tells you where you are without lying. It gives direction on where you are going.

In the Garden of Eden, Eve's conscience said, "God said do not eat of this tree." Satan's rebuttal was, "You will surely not die. Go ahead and eat of the fruit." Satan told Eve that the forbidden fruit was delicious.

The devil is always offering something that he does not have. He said the fruit would be enlightening to the soul. What Satan did not tell Eve was that her rebellion would be devastating to the human spirit. The rebellion would alienate her from the Most High God. It would bring pain in childbirth and sorrow to her and all women who would ever live on earth.

When a person realizes he is in trouble, his conscience begins to assist him. "Remember that thing you did!" Then you pray, "Oh, God, forgive me."

Why was your conscience so alive? Because you were in trouble. Men in foxholes during war make all kinds of promises and commitments to God. Men and women in hospitals make new resolutions, conscience resolutions. A man who used to come to my church in South Bend was in the hospital. When I went up to see him, he gave his heart to Jesus on the hospital bed. He told me, "I almost went to hell over fishing on Sunday." Over and over he said, "I almost went to hell over a six-inch fish."

The human conscience has the built-in authority to convict or approve your actions. Your conscience can approve of your deeds or expose them.

Conscience can make you aware of real needs. The conscience is a policeman. It is a watchman over your soul. Conscience is a court of appeals, evaluating the decisions you have made.

This generation has a conscience burned out as if by a hot iron, and many people do not know right from wrong.

Through the reading of the Word, your conscience will produce conviction of sin. Without conscience there is no conviction.

You cannot imagine what goes on inside the hearts of men and women who live dishonestly with their mates. Their consciences will accuse them for the rest of their lives. There is no medicine to heal the conscience. Drugs bring only temporary relief.

The human conscience can bring a person from hopelessness to the Most High God. When your conscience tells you that you really need help, Christ is the Helper.

Paul wrote in 1 Timothy 3:9, *"Holding the mystery of the faith in a pure conscience."* Your conscience functions by the mystery of faith. The human conscience, when born again, is taught how to please God by the Holy Spirit and through the Word of God. It functions through the newborn spirit dwelling within you. Paul called this *"the mystery of faith."* Faith guides the conscience into making spiritual decisions rather than carnal and sinful ones.

Second Corinthians 1:12 says, *"For our rejoicing is this, the testimony of our conscience."* The testimony of your conscience witnesses to what kind of person you are. The apostle Paul declared that his conscience gave witness to the simplicity and the sincerity of his ministry to people.

Paul said, "I have a better witness and testimony inside me. His name is conscience, and he is a good witness upwardly toward God. He has a good witness outwardly toward you. He has a good witness inwardly, inside myself. I feel good inside." That is very important.

The Bible speaks to us about holding on to our conscience and getting a grasp on it. First Timothy 1:19 says, *"Holding faith, and a good conscience; which some having put away concerning faith have made shipwreck."* You have to keep a good, clean conscience that is spiritual and joyful unto the Lord. We must guard our consciences like treasure. We must hold on to a good conscience.

First Timothy 4:2 says, *"Speaking lies in hypocrisy; having their conscience seared with a hot iron."*

Paul spoke of an impaired or abused conscience. Your conscience can beat on the door of your heart and be refused entrance. He can make your brain restless at night because you did not do what was right during the day. The human conscience can be seared with a hot iron. It can be burned out. It can become so calloused that even if you committed murder, your conscience would not bother you.

A man's convictions are clear by his conscience revealing his real person. Your conscience is like your shadow. It is always there.

Man has to learn to live with his conscience because the conscience is the scale of eternal justice.

32
Does God Have a Conscience?

---◆◆◆---

And the LORD said, I have surely seen the affliction of my people which are in Egypt, and have heard their cry by reason of their taskmasters; for I know their sorrows; and I am come down to deliver them out of the hand of the Egyptians, and to bring them up out of that land unto a good land and a large, unto a land flowing with milk and honey; unto the place of the Canaanites, and the Hittites, and the Amorites, and the Perizzites, and the Hivites, and the Jebusites. Now therefore, behold, the cry of the children of Israel is come unto me: and I have also seen the oppression wherewith the Egyptians oppress them.

(Exodus 3:7–9)

*W*e can see clearly in this Scripture that God is conscious of earthly conditions. He is conscious of human persons. He sees our sorrows and hurts. He hears our cries. Conscience moves a person. When a person's conscience begins to flow in a certain direction, whether it is anger or love, his whole being flows in that direction.

God gave man a conscience, and man must use this conscience to direct his own life, decisions, and choices before God. The Bible tells us in Genesis, chapter 1, that man is created in the image and likeness of God. He possesses God-conscience, or God-consciousness. God must have a conscience, or man could not be God-conscious. Conscience evaluates moral conduct. God has an amazing and tremendous conscience. God understands feelings that have never been represented outwardly and words that have never been spoken. He understands man's innermost feelings. God knows how to deal with conscience in your life or mine.

Is God absolute conscience, or is He above conscience? A king may be above his laws, but if that king disrespects his own laws, his subjects will also disrespect the laws, and his kingdom will deteriorate. Soon he will be overcome by a stronger nation. God's conscience is not above law. He operates the moral fabric of the universe on His consciousness.

In Genesis 1:26 God said,

> Let us make man in our image, after our likeness: and let them have dominion over the fish of the sea, and over the fowl of the air, and over the cattle, and over all the earth, and over every creeping thing that creepeth upon the earth.

It was through His conscience that God conceived man in His own likeness. God delighted in His creation, and when God created His universe, He looked upon it and said it was good. The consciousness of God flowed out of the things He had created. He was conscious that they were good.

> And God blessed them [Adam and Eve], and God said unto them, Be fruitful, and multiply, and replenish the earth, and subdue it: and have dominion over the fish of the sea, and over the fowl of the air, and over every living thing that moveth upon the earth. And God said, Behold, I have given you every herb bearing seed, which is upon the face of all the earth,

and every tree, in the which is the fruit of a tree yield-
ing seed; to you it shall be for meat. And to every beast
of the earth, and to every fowl of the air, and to every
thing that creepeth upon the earth, wherein there is
life, I have given every green herb for meat: and it was
so. (Genesis 1:28–30)

We see the consciousness of God in His creative works, in His choice of what He did and where He placed the sovereignty over planet Earth. He placed the dominion over all His creation in the human person. He placed the scale of eternal justice, called conscience, inside him. The conscience, with the knowledge of good and evil, became awakened and came into mighty activity at the time of transgression. Adam's conscience had to decide which of these to follow.

We see conscience working strongly after the Fall. Genesis 3:8 says, *"And they heard the voice of the LORD God walking in the garden in the cool of the day: and Adam and his wife hid themselves from the presence of the LORD God amongst the trees of the garden."* Without a conscience they would not have hidden themselves. They were smitten by their consciences working in their minds, emotions, and wills.

Conscience is a soulical power and function. It cannot be taken out. If a person goes to hell, his conscience will be there. Jesus told a story about a rich man in Luke 15. Even though he was in hell, he had a conscience bearing witness to the life that he lived on this earth. You are not going to lose your conscience. You are going to keep it for eternity. For that reason it is subject to the laws of God. You must live in subjection to the Most High in order to have eternal peace and joy.

Genesis 6:1–3 says,

> *And it came to pass, when men began to multiply on the face of the earth, and daughters were born unto them, that the sons of God saw the daughters of men that they were fair; and they took them wives of all which they chose. And the LORD said, My spirit shall not always strive with man, for that he also is flesh: yet his days shall be an hundred and twenty years.*

Man could have lived forever in the Garden of Eden. After Adam sinned, his life span was limited to about a thousand years. God saw that man learned to sin so quickly that He reduced their days nearly a thousand years to around one hundred and twenty years. Later He reduced them again to about seventy years. Man has had his years reduced because of his rebellion against God and not paying attention to his conscience.

What happened when the sons of Elohim married regular women of Adam's seed? Verse 4 continues, *"There were giants in the earth in those days."* The sons of Elohim fathered giants. There may have been men whose heads were three feet across. They had six fingers on each hand and six toes on each foot. They may have been ten feet tall and weighed five or six hundred pounds. They were probably brutes who growled like lions. They were not human; they were something other than human.

"And God saw that the wickedness of man was great in the earth, and that every imagination of the thoughts of his heart was only evil continually" (Genesis 6:5). That is what conscience will do for you. God saw and understood the whole situation through the powers of His conscience.

God said He repented that He had even made a man on the earth. It grieved Him in His heart. That is conscience! Jehovah said,

I will destroy man whom I have created from the face of the earth; both man, and beast, and the creeping thing, and the fowls of the air; for it repenteth me that I have made them.   (Genesis 6:7)

All this came from rebellion, which is a feature of the conscience inside a man.

Verse 8 says, *"But Noah found grace in the eyes of the LORD."* Earth has had three great priesthoods. The first was the priesthood of the sons of God, who were called the priests of Melchizedek. The Word of God tells us about them in Hebrews, chapters 5–7.

Hebrews 5:6–7, speaking of Jesus, says,

Thou art a priest for ever after the order of Melchisedec. Who in the days of his flesh, when he had offered up prayers and supplications with strong crying and tears unto him that was able to save him from death, and was heard in that he feared.

This reveals to us the great conscience of God. He had to work with great wickedness from Adam right down to Noah—nearly two thousand years.

God had great feelings toward sin and righteousness, good and bad in those early times of man. Conscience came straight out of the Garden of Eden. God still has a conscience that is working toward you and toward all humanity, right now.

Genesis 18:20–21 tells us about a city called Sodom.

And the LORD said, Because the cry of Sodom and Gomorrah is great, and because their sin is very grievous; I will go down now, and see whether they have done altogether according to the cry of it, which is come unto me; and if not, I will know.

Here we see God's consciousness toward the great city of Sodom.

Moses was very aware of the consciousness of God. God saw Israel's suffering in Egypt; He heard their cry; He saw their taskmasters. In Exodus 3:7 God said, *"I know their sorrows."* That is the function of God's conscience.

God delivered the Israelites out of Egypt and brought them to the Red Sea.

> *And the Egyptians shall know that I am the* Lord, *when I have gotten me honour upon Pharaoh, upon his chariots, and upon his horsemen. And the angel of God, which went before the camp of Israel, removed and went behind them; and the pillar of the cloud went from before their face, and stood behind them: and it came between the camp of the Egyptians and the camp of Israel; and it was a cloud and darkness to them, but it gave light by night to these: so that the one came not near the other all the night.*
>
> (Exodus 14:18–20)

The Egyptians wanted to cross on the dry seabed, but they could not. God overthrew the Egyptians completely. God had seen what had happened to the Israeli people, and He said, "I'll do something about it." His conscience was stirred, and God dealt with that situation.

God knows good and bad. Though He is pure and good and holy, through His consciousness He understands unholiness and impurity.

God's conscience was moved in the desert toward Israel when they worshipped the golden calf. He was angry about it. Whenever they did wrong during those forty years of desert wanderings, the conscience of God was stirred up toward them.

God also has a conscience toward you. He sees what you do every day. He understands your motivations on the inside. God knows when your lips speak one thing and your heart believes another. He judges you by His conscience.

David was a great man who understood the consciousness of God. Second Samuel 23:10 says,

> *He arose, and smote the Philistines until his hand was weary, and his hand clave unto the sword: and the LORD wrought a great victory that day; and the people returned after him only to spoil.*

First Samuel 25:31 says,

> *That this shall be no grief unto thee, nor offence of heart unto my lord, either that thou hast shed blood causeless, or that my lord hath avenged himself: but when the LORD shall have dealt well with my lord, then remember thine handmaid.*

David had been mistreated and he was about to kill Nabal when Nabal's wife said, "Oh, don't do that; he is not worth it." She brought his God-consciousness alive within him.

When we study the Psalms, we realize that David was a person who strongly understood the conscience of God. In fact, the whole Bible is a picture to us of the conscience of God. Every word in the Bible represents God-consciousness. What does God say about this? How does God feel about this matter? What will God do in this case? The Bible is God's conscience toward sin, good, and people.

I believe the seven dispensations of time were given to man in order to let his conscience come alive to God. God, through His conscious spirit, gave man these seven opportunities to know and serve Him.

I believe that Christ is actually the conscience of God on the earth. How does God feel? Look at Jesus, and you can see how God feels. He is an image of the Father. How does God make judgment? Observe Jesus. To the woman caught in adultery, He said, *"Neither do I condemn thee: go and sin no more"* (John 8:11). Jesus still loved her. Christ and His conscious acts reveal to us the conscience of God. He is the beautiful image of the Most High and how God feels about everything.

The New Jerusalem, the eternal city of God, may be the very conscience of God. The ultimate feeling of God will be in the building, making, and creating of the New Jerusalem. It will be His perfect restoration. The New Jerusalem will be the fulfillment of God's total joy. The New Jerusalem will be the embodiment of what God determined by His feeling and by His conscience.

In the heart of the Almighty, conscience is the scale of eternal justice. God has a conscience; if He did not, man would not be on the face of this earth.

33
The Dispensation of Conscience

◆●◆

*T*here was a period of time when conscience was the law of the land. It was the only law men had. It is remarkable that God created a dispensation called Conscience.

When Adam and Eve were expelled from the Garden of Eden, God removed them from the Dispensation of Innocence and brought them into an era called the Dispensation of Conscience. Human consciousness had been born in them through eating the fruit of the Tree of Knowledge of Good and Evil. They now had to live under the new law that they had created, the law of obedience by conscience. Their minds, emotions, and wills—the areas of the functioning of the conscience— would tell them how they should live before God.

The Dispensation of Conscience was a long one— one thousand six hundred and fifty-six years. It began at the door of Eden after Adam's debacle and continued until the Flood covered the earth in Noah's day.

The human life span was changed in this dispensation. God said, *"My spirit shall not always strive with man"* (Genesis 6:3). God shortened man's life span, which was almost a thousand years, to one hundred and twenty years. That is a tremendous change.

Adam volitionally decided to choose his own way rather than God's way. He had a personal determination to do something that God did not want him to do. A power called human consciousness awakened in him to determine between good and evil. Since that time, every moral act of man was governed by the conscience inside him. This began the remarkable period of time known as the Dispensation of Conscience. Man had no laws. He had no governors. He lived by the power of his own conscience saying, "This is good; that is bad." He was ruled only by inner feelings during this Dispensation of Conscience. Man had total freedom to make his own decisions. After the debacle in Eden, God said, "I will speak to man through his conscience and converse with him through his inner man."

Adam and Eve had two sons. One was named Cain, the other Abel. The devil put it in the heart of Cain to kill his brother, Abel. The devil said, "One of these will bruise my head." He thought the first one born would be the redeemer, so he caused Cain to murder Abel through rebellion. This damned his conscience. As long as Cain lived, he had a terrible conscience. There are people who commit suicide because their consciences hammer away at them until they cannot stand it.

God showed Adam that a lamb must be slain for a sacrifice. Abel obeyed this law that God had laid down, but his brother Cain would not. As Abel brought his offering of the lamb, Cain brought his vegetable sacrifice from the field. God said, "I cannot accept your offering; only blood can cover a trespass. The life of the flesh is in the blood." Satan said, "I have destroyed the program of God. I caused Cain to destroy Abel, so I cannot be hurt and my head cannot be bruised. If I can infiltrate the seed of the woman, there will never be any pure seed to produce a world savior." This was an awful thing to try to perpetrate upon the human race and the seed of Adam!

There have been three priesthoods in the history of the human race. The first one was the Melchizedek priesthood, which we have already described. This priesthood functioned during the period called Conscience. The people had preachers who reminded them that they should not live bad lives. Even the priesthood fell into sin. It lost its conscience.

The genealogy of this period is not very exciting. It says that they were born, lived, and died. When you read it, you say, "Is that all a person can do: be born, live, and die? Is it true that all you can expect is a tombstone?" However, when history comes to the man named Enoch, the pattern changes. In only a few verses his whole life story is told, but he changed history! Genesis 5:22 says, *"And Enoch walked with God."* This was the dispensation in which God desired men to walk with Him personally. He wanted to deal with them on a personal basis of conscience.

Enoch walked with God so perfectly that when he was three hundred and sixty-five years old, God took him to heaven without his dying. What a miracle! Enoch was sixty-five years old when his son Methuselah was born. Adam, the great-great-great-grandfather of Methuselah, was about six hundred years old. Then Adam had time to tell Methuselah how he had lived in the Garden, and how Eve ate him out of house and home.

Enoch was a prophet of God. One of his prophecies was in the naming of his own son. The name *Methuselah* means, "At his death judgment comes." That was an awful name to give a child. Everyone who knew him would try to keep him alive, because they knew that at his death, judgment would come. What amazes me is that this man lived longer than any human has ever lived. He lived nine hundred and sixty-nine years, because God did not want to judge anyone. The year

Methuselah died was the same year the Flood came. The Flood terminated the Dispensation of Conscience. God was waiting for man to become good, clean, and pure. That was what the Dispensation of Conscience was all about. It was time to live for God.

The reason Methuselah lived so long was that God did not want to send that flood of water upon the earth. Noah had the ark ready. It was the mercy of God that held the rain back. God said, "I will give you one more chance. The day that Methuselah dies I will send judgment upon the earth because his name means 'At death judgment comes.'" God gave Methuselah an extra year until he finally lived longer than every other human who had ever lived on planet Earth. This reveals the great mercy, love, and conscience of God. God's conscience goes out to you in your weakness and failings. God wants to bring you back to Himself no matter how much you have transgressed against Him. God is love. He does not want to judge mankind, but He must.

After the Flood, God started all over again with a new dispensation called Human Government, when men checked on other men. The Dispensation of Conscience terminated at the Flood in the time of Noah, and it is gone forever. God never moves in reverse; God only moves forward. There will never be a period of innocence as there was in the Garden of Eden. There will never be a period called Conscience as there was for almost two thousand years. Christ has now accomplished the first promise in the Bible: *"And I will put enmity between thee and the woman, and between thy seed and her seed; it shall bruise thy head, and thou shalt bruise his heel"* (Genesis 3:15).

We now live in the Dispensation of Grace, when the Lord Jesus speaks to man through his heart and

the Word of God, the Bible. The Dispensation of Conscience was a very beautiful time, but it is terminated.
We live under a different agreement with God. First
John 1:9 says, *"If we confess our sins, he is faithful and just
to forgive us our sins, and to cleanse us from all unrighteous-
ness."*

Only a very few great people lived in the time
of Conscience. One was Enoch, who was translated to
heaven. Another was Methuselah. We do not know if
he was good or bad. We just know that he lived a long
time. Enoch broke through the wall of unbelief and
walked with God. What an achievement! Methuselah
was celebrated in that his father Enoch prophesied over
him the day he was born. He was the oldest man who
ever lived. Noah, by his righteousness and good conscience, saved the whole world.

A few great men lived in the Dispensation of Conscience, but not many. In these last days it might be
the same again. There may not be many people with a
great conscience inside them.

The regulation of conscience in those days was
what you might call a free moral agency or a self-acting
entity. The scale of eternal justice moved on man's
behalf, and God did everything that He could to bring
man into a place of fulfillment, peace, and joy in Himself. This dispensation ended in defeat for man because
he did not obey the laws of his dispensation. They had
nothing written on stone; they had nothing written on
paper; they had no judges sitting to judge them. Their
whole lives were built upon their consciences.

34
Human Conscience without God

---◆●◆---

*N*ow *the end of the commandment is charity out of a pure heart, and of a good conscience, and of faith unfeigned"* (1 Timothy 1:5). It is possible for humans to have a good conscience before God and man. Man can stand before them, making the right decisions, doing the right things, and having a good conscience.

Verse 19 says, *"Holding faith, and a good conscience; which some having put away concerning faith have made shipwreck."* You must hold on to a good conscience. The human conscience is a divine attribute possessed by the soulical man on this earth.

We do not know who else has a conscience in the universe, but we know that God does. The Bible reveals that. We know that man does. We also know that animals do not have a conscience. They are not responsible for their actions because they do not possess a conscience. Man has this attribute. Walking in holy consciousness, the human person yields his conscience to the laws of the Most High and to the Holy Spirit of God.

In rebellion, through following the devil against the Most High God, the human conscience is without divine guidance. This means it is motivated by demonic or human forces.

The first sin ever committed on planet Earth created a guilty conscience. In Genesis 3:10, Adam confessed, *"I heard thy voice in the garden, and I was afraid, because I was naked; and I hid myself."* A conscience not motivated by God caused man to be afraid. The first thing Adam said was, *"I was afraid."* Fear comes because of a warped conscience. With a conscience in relationship and attitude toward God, a person is not fearful. He is strong, brave, and courageous. However, a conscience not motivated by the Most High is a seedbed for fear.

Adam also said, *"I was naked."* A human conscience without God is disrobed of its holiness, purity, and virginity. It discovers itself naked before the Most High. The human conscience without God is fearful of the unknown. Adam did not know what was going to happen to him. He was afraid and hid himself from reality, from fellowship with the One who had created him. The human conscience without God does not understand the unknown. It knows it has made the wrong decision, and the insides of a human being become fearful.

We have what we call the voice of conscience. It all began in the beginning of the Bible. Not much has changed in the last six thousand years. The Lord said to Cain in Genesis 4:9-10, *"Where is Abel thy brother? And he said, I know not: Am I my brother's keeper? And he said, What hast thou done? the voice of thy brother's blood crieth unto me from the ground."* This is the voice of conscience.

When the people of Israel were in Egypt, their voices of weeping and hurting persecution cried out. Their consciences cried out, and God, with His consciousness, perceived it. He said, "I hear it, and I will come down and do something about it." We have the voice of conscience crying. A voice cries for those who do not have sufficient clothing or housing, and God will hear their cry. God will hear your cry if you will cry out to Him and say, "This is not right. I want help."

In 1 Kings 21:19 we read about a king and his queen who did not do right.

> *And thou shalt speak unto him, saying, Thus saith the* Lord, *Hast thou killed, and also taken possession? And thou shalt speak unto him, saying, Thus saith the* Lord, *In the place where dogs licked the blood of Naboth shall dogs lick thy blood, even thine.*

Queen Jezebel stole Naboth's vineyard and had him killed by false accusers. Naboth's blood cried out and God said, "In the same place where he died, you will die. You left him there for the dogs to eat his flesh, and the same thing will happen to you."

We discover in the Bible that when David sinned, Nathan the prophet came and said, "You are the man; you are guilty," and David's conscience was activated. In Psalm 51 you will find that David was beaten down by his own insides. He came to God with great contrition and said, "Forgive me; I am sorry; please forgive me." He was a man who found his way back to God.

The voice of conscience comes in many ways. When I was a young man living in the state of Mississippi, I was told a story about a logging pond in the town of Laurel. Two men were working in the logging pond, taking the logs, putting them under the water, then pulling them out onto a big crawler. From there they would go inside the mill to be sawed into all kinds of timber. After they were dried, the timbers were sent out to build houses all over the world.

One day one of the men laughed and said, "In this pond ten years ago, I planted a grain of rice and it never did grow." The other man began to think. Finally he said, "There was a man named Rice who used to live here ten years ago and disappeared. His family never knew what happened to him." He went to the police and said, "I would like you to drag the bottom of that millpond. A man told me that he planted a grain of rice in it ten years ago. If you will look back through the newspapers, you will find that ten years ago a man named Rice disappeared."

The police took their instruments and dragged the bottom of the pond and they brought up a skeleton with a chain wrapped around it! When the police presented the bones and the chain to the logger, he confessed that he had been working with Mr. Rice and that he knocked him unconscious, wrapped a log chain around him, sinking him to the bottom of the pond. He said, "I could not stand it any longer. Every night, every day, this thing was on my mind. I could not stand it!"

A person without God needs the consciousness of God. Your conscience will cry out to you. You have to say, "God, I want a converted conscience. I want a conscience toward God and not a conscience without God." A conscience without God will destroy you. It will beat you to pieces. There are people in the insane asylums right now because their consciences have beaten them into that place.

The human conscience without God is fearful of the unknown, of the future, and of coming judgment.

The voice of conscience cries out to people. It cries out to God. It has a force and power. Even though the man was dead, the conscience still cried out.

God calls the unconverted conscience defiled and dirty. First Corinthians 8:7 says, *"Howbeit there is not in every man that knowledge: for some with conscience of the idol unto this hour eat it as a thing offered unto an idol; and their conscience being weak is defiled."*

Sin and rebellion will always bring defilement or uncleanness. God said the defiled conscience is a weak conscience. You can make your conscience stronger by working on it.

The human conscience without God is the consciousness of sin. It is the conscience that produces the sense of guiltiness before God.

Animal sacrifice could not heal consciousness of sin. Jesus came so that conscious thought could distinguish what is morally good from what is morally wrong if we are righteous and live before God. A good conscience can commend us. God wants us to live before Him in uprightness.

Acts 26:9 is an interesting Scripture. *"I verily thought with myself, that I ought to do many things contrary to the name of Jesus of Nazareth."* Here we learn that a person can have an ignorant conscience. Paul had been trained that people with the wrong religion ought to die. He put Christians in jail. He stood by and watched as Stephen was stoned. He went to Damascus to put the whole church in jail. In all this, his conscience was ignorant of what he was doing wrong. That may be true in many situations.

Romans 10:2 says, *"For I bear them record that they have a zeal of God, but not according to knowledge."* Their consciences were in a state of ignorance. When conscience comes into a state of wisdom and knowledge, it guides man the way he should be guided.

Psalm 40:11–12 says,

Withhold not thou thy tender mercies from me, O LORD: let thy lovingkindness and thy truth continually preserve me. For innumerable evils have compassed me about: mine iniquities have taken hold upon me, so that I am not able to look up; they are more than the hairs of mine head: therefore my heart faileth me.

Here was a guilty conscience crying out for mercy. The psalmist was telling how his conscience was beating him to death. His conscience was actually destroying him. He needed God to forgive him and give him a clean conscience so he could live the right way. If you will seek God, He can heal your conscience. He can heal the misdoings and misgivings of the past. He can make your conscience new.

In Matthew 27:3–5 we read,

Then Judas, which had betrayed him, when he saw that he was condemned, repented himself, and brought again the thirty pieces of silver to the chief priests and elders, saying, I have sinned in that I have betrayed the innocent blood. And they said, What is that to us? see thou to that. And he cast down the pieces of silver in the temple, and departed, and went and hanged himself.

Acts 1:25 says, *"Judas by transgression fell."* He was not predestined to do this. He did not have an overpowering situation from outside him making him do it. He wanted to do it. Judas' conscience drove him to suicide. That was an evil, sinful conscience. He took his own life. People never commit suicide with a good conscience. They always have griefs, sorrows, and hurts they cannot overcome. They say, "The only way out is to kill myself." It is not the way out! The way out is for Jesus to come into your heart and make you a new creature.

First Timothy 4:1–2 has a very familiar word that I would like you to hear again. It says,

Now the Spirit speaketh expressly, that in the latter times some shall depart from the faith, giving heed to seducing spirits, and doctrines of devils; speaking lies in hypocrisy; having their conscience seared with a hot iron.

This means that you can burn out your conscience. You can bruise your conscience until it ceases to function. You can keep putting down your conscience until nothing is there. There are people who kill in cold blood and never think anything about it. They need an operation on their consciences. Judas missed it. His conscience drove him the wrong way because he was without Christ.

Peter's conscience was different. Even though he had sinned and blasphemed, he wept with bitterness and said, "I would like to get to Christ and be forgiven." That is exactly what happened to him.

"Knowing therefore the terror of the Lord, we persuade men; but we are made manifest unto God; and I trust also are made manifest in your consciences" (2 Corinthians 5:11). Paul was saying, "I want you in your conscience to know that I am a good man. I am speaking truth. I am speaking of God. I want you to believe that and to understand it." The Amplified version reads,

We must all appear and be revealed as we are before the judgment seat of Christ, so that each one may receive (his pay) according to what he has done in the body, whether good or evil, (considering what his purpose and motive have been, and what he has achieved, been busy with and given himself and his attention to accomplishing). Therefore, being conscious of fearing the Lord with respect and reverence, we seek to win people over—to persuade them. But what sort of persons we are is plainly recognized and thoroughly

understood by God, and I hope that it is plainly recog-
nized and understood also by your consciences—that
is, by your inborn discernment.

(2 Corinthians 5:10-11)

Another version reads,

For we must all appear before the judgment seat of
Christ, that each one may receive what is due him for
the things done while in the body, whether good or
bad. Since, then, we know what it is to fear the Lord,
we try to persuade men. What we are is plain to God,
and I hope it is also plain to your conscience. (NIV)

When you come to the Lord Jesus Christ and confess your sins, He puts a new conscience in you. The
Bible says, *"If we confess our sins, he is faithful and just to*
forgive us our sins, and to cleanse us from all unrighteous-
ness" (1 John 1:9). At that point in time, you receive a
new conscience. Your old conscience passes away, and
you receive a born-again conscience. An evil conscience
breeds evil. A bad conscience breeds demonic effects.
Every unbeliever has a conscience that has been hurt
and, like Adam, is hiding from God. An evil conscience
is fearful and tormenting. When you come to Jesus
Christ and your sins are wiped away, you have a new
life in Him. A newborn conscience dwells within you.
All the nightmares of yesterday are gone. The sorrows
of a heavy conscience are gone. The blood of Jesus
Christ, God's Son, cleanses you from an evil conscience.
God can pull the drapes of yesterday and give you a
brand-new future with a beautiful, new, magnificent
conscience! Receive it! Accept it! Walk in Him! You will
always be glad that you did!

35
Reborn Conscience

*I*t is possible to have operations within you that you do not understand. When this is the case, you do not know when you are working with God or not. You do not know how to direct your inner being. It is necessary to learn of these things; it is of prime importance to know about conscience. Let us consider the reborn, saved, or converted conscience.

The human conscience fell from grace with the sin and rebellion of Adam in the Garden of Eden. At that time the human conscience fell into disrepute.

All sinners have a conscience. Hebrews 10:22 says, *"Let us draw near with a true heart in full assurance of faith, having our hearts sprinkled from an evil conscience."* The conscience of man became evil through transgression. It was not evil before the Fall.

It is possible to change the human conscience. In your born-again experience many things change—your mind, emotions, and conscience change when you are born again.

The conscience can become pure only by the blood of Jesus. It cannot be cleansed by resolutions. You cannot talk yourself out of it or go to a psychiatrist and have him give you reasons out of your past.

There is only one way a human conscience can be made holy. Hebrews 9:14 tells us, *"How much more shall the blood of Christ, who through the eternal Spirit offered himself without spot to God, purge your conscience from dead works to serve the living God?"* Only Christ can produce the reborn conscience.

Hebrew 13:18 says, *"Pray for us: for we trust we have a good conscience."* The only way to have a good conscience is for the blood of Jesus Christ, God's Son, to cleanse us from all our sins. Then we do not have that evil conscience, but a conscience that is holy and good unto God.

The reborn conscience is so exciting. In many countries, my wife and I had observed the miracle of the rebirth. We had seen men and women who were living together without a marriage because the wedding certificates from the government cost so much that they could not afford them. The couples were just living together without the paper, but they were true to each other. They had lived together ten or fifteen years, but were not officially married. When they got saved, inside them they would say, "This is not right. We have ten children, but we are not married." When they were born again, something inside them said, "Conform to God's commandments!"

As long as families are living in sin, adultery does not condemn them. When their conscience becomes purged by the blood of Jesus, they receive a good conscience before God.

It is beautiful to see a once rebellious conscience become reborn and to witness the whole inside of a person change.

Let's look at the story Jesus gave in Luke 15:17, *"When* [the prodigal] *came to himself."* It is hard to know what that means. When he tired of the way he was living, he realized that home was not so bad after all. When he got tired of living with pigs, he came to himself and said, "Now, wait a minute. In my father's house there are hired servants. There is bread enough for everyone and plenty left over. I am perishing with hunger. I am a son, but I am perishing with hunger while my father's servants are throwing away food." That was the awakening of conscience within him.

Verse 18 says, *"I will arise and go to my father, and will say unto him, Father, I have sinned."* That is what salvation is all about. It was hard for him to say, *"I have sinned against heaven, and before thee, and am no more worthy to be called thy son"* (vv. 18–19). This was the miracle of the soulical person, and especially this prodigal son, in the rebirth of a new life.

Home became a desirable place. He did not like it when he walked off and said, "I am glad to get away from this place. I am tired of seeing Mom and Dad. You are old fuddy-duddies anyway. You are so far out of time that you do not know what is going on in the world. I am leaving here!" When his conscience came alive, the first thing he said was, "The place I left was desirable."

The same thing happens to sinners when they are born again. Before they were born again, they did not like church. Afterwards, you cannot get them to go home.

This prodigal son had entered into a higher state of appreciation. That is what happens to a sinner. He does not like the singing, praising, praying, or preaching. In fact, he does not like anything about God. When Jesus comes into his heart, he has a new appreciation of God, the Word of God, and the worship hour. He has a new appreciation of everything related to heaven, God, and eternity. That is what it means to have a renewed and reborn conscience!

The prodigal realized his miserable condition. He realized that he had been in the state of rebellion against his father. He confessed it freely.

That is when the conscience is really working, cleaning up the past, cleaning out the mud and the mess, and letting you see that a pigsty is not a parlor. Sinners do not know the difference so they play in the pigsty. When they let Jesus into their hearts, they say, "I cannot stand this mess anymore. I do not even like these 'pigs' I have been running around with."

Romans 13:5 says, *"Wherefore ye must needs be subject, not only for wrath, but also for conscience sake."* It is not easy to be subject to others. Rebellion is a normal thing for the unregenerate. Sometimes rebellion even gets into believers' lives. You can be a rebel at work. You can be a rebel at home. You can be a rebel at church. When the conscience comes alive in Jesus, your old conscience is changed or reborn.

We must keep our consciences functioning because conscience is the moral and spiritual guide of our destiny.

I have been in countries where I would not drink coffee for the simple reason that Christians in that country thought drinking coffee was a sin. So I drank water, and that is all right with me. I want to live, wherever I am in the world, in a way that will help people go to heaven and not tear them down.

The apostle Paul said in 1 Corinthians 8:13, *"Wherefore, if meat make my brother to offend, I will eat no flesh while the world standeth, lest I make my brother to offend."* Paul was functioning in the area of conscience.

Today the church needs the reborn conscience to make its way through the world, seeking to win many to God and not hurting anyone. Your conscience is an antenna that bends one way or the other, telling you to do this or not to do that and to be careful not to offend other people.

One of the greatest powers of conscience is prayer. I could speak harshly to my wife and feel rather good about it. When I begin to pray the Lord says, "Why are you so nasty in your speech?" I might retort, "I had my rights." God's firm answer is, "No, you did not have any rights. Go say you are sorry." The matter seemed all right until my conscience got quiet in an attitude of worship. Your conscience can purge, cleanse, and work for you.

Prayer attains a high degree of sensitivity in order that we might, like the apostle Paul said, "walk before God and before man with a good conscience."

The word *purge* can mean "to purify, clean up, or separate." It means to separate one thing from another. It means to wash out and take away the impurities. Jesus wants to remove guilt from the human person. On the other hand, if you talk to a man who works with trees, *purge* means to cut off twigs and cut back branches. Sometimes a branch might grow out too fast and it needs to be cut back. The Lord does this kind of purging so that we can produce better spiritual fruit.

You can teach the Word of God to some people, and they will do the opposite. It is amazing that you can teach people, and they will go shooting out a little branch before they are ready for it. Then God has to trim it back. You can do the right thing at the wrong time. You can do a good thing at a bad time. If you wait until God does it, it will be so easy, good, successful, and blessed.

It is the same way with getting married. You can get married at the right time or the wrong time. I always thought I had no business getting married until I was able to provide a house to live in. One of the first things I did when my wife and I were married was to buy a house. We did not live in it much, but we had a house. We were never stranded; we could always go home. To marry a girl and strand her is not the right way to begin life together. If a young man would work more diligently and make full preparation, he might have a lot more happiness after marriage.

My wife and I were married for nearly fifty years. She never had to worry about where her food was coming from or if she would have a place to stay.

The apostle Paul talked about conscience more than anyone else in the Bible. He was very conscious of conscience, maybe because he was trained in the ways of the Greeks and the concept of conscience was a strong thought in their culture.

In Acts 24:16 Paul said, *"Herein do I exercise myself* [I move myself; I give a lot of activity in the area of having], *to have always a conscience void of offence toward God."*

Paul said, "My conscience will not offend God." Paul further said, "I will not allow an offense toward men." He was striving for a good conscience toward God and man.

In the New Testament, the word *offense* is used as something that provokes prejudice or becomes a hindrance. Offense can sometimes, in itself, be a good thing.

For example, you may say, "I am a holy person. I will not drink alcohol." This may be an offense to some people. I have had people tell me, "If your rejoicing was not so strong, I would worship with you." We offended them by rejoicing in Jesus, but we cannot stop.

The greatest lesson to learn from a conscience void of offense is that we must do nothing whereby we would cause a brother in Christ to stumble or fall. Daniel did not want to offend anyone in Babylon, but when he prayed he offended the whole empire.

In Acts 23:1 the apostle Paul said, *"Men and brethren, I have lived in all good conscience before God until this day."* The Amplified version says, *"Then Paul, gazing earnestly at the council (Sanhedrin), said, Brethren, I have lived before God doing my duty with a perfectly good conscience until this very day."*

Paul had a good conscience about everything that he had done. In 1 Timothy 1:5 he said, *"Now the end of the commandment is charity out of a pure heart, and of a good conscience, and of faith unfeigned."* All of us must "hold faith and a good conscience." If you do not hold on to a good conscience, you can lose it. *"Which some having put away concerning faith have made shipwreck"* (1 Timothy 1:19).

I have a good conscience. I have never hurt anyone to get anything that I have.

First Peter 3:16 says, *"Having a good conscience; that, whereas they speak evil of you, as of evildoers, they may be ashamed that falsely accuse your good conversation in Christ."* Enemies of God can falsely accuse your good conscience in Christ. You can have a good conscience and people will misunderstand you completely. How glad I am to have a good conscience with a mystery of faith surrounding it.

Second Timothy 1:3 says, *"I thank God, whom I serve from my forefathers with pure conscience, that without ceasing I have remembrance of thee in my prayers night and day."* A pure conscience is one that has been cleansed. It has not only been purged, cut off, and separated, but it is pure. You have to be born again in order to be the person God wants you to be. If you will do that, you will stand before God, and He will praise you for it.

Paul said in 2 Corinthians 4:2, *"But have renounced the hidden things of dishonesty, not walking in craftiness, nor handling the word of God deceitfully; but by manifestation of the truth commending ourselves to every man's conscience in the sight of God."* We should commend ourselves to people through conscience.

A Christian can endure grief, suffering wrongfully, because of his conscience toward God. The reborn conscience can bear sorrow. It can bear hurt when others say, "I cannot stand it." A pure conscience can stand it.

John 8:9 reads, *"And they which heard it, being convicted by their own conscience, went out one by one, beginning at the eldest, even unto the last: and Jesus was left alone, and the woman standing in the midst."*

These men had stones in their hands. Their consciences told them, "Stone her!" Jesus awakened within them a new conscience. He said, "You without sin, cast the first stone."

They began to look at one another and say, "You know, I am guilty, and you are guilty." They dropped their stones on the ground, and one by one they walked away, awakened by a conscience. The Bible says they were convicted by their own consciences. When they saw the attitude of Jesus, they had an awakening of a conscience that they did not have before.

There are two judgments before us. One is the judgment seat of Christ, which is just for believers, and the other is the Great White Throne judgment. At this latter judgment, only sinners are judged. At both judgments, every wrong thing that people have done and justified to themselves will be weighed on the scale of eternal justice—the conscience.

This means our conscience needs to be purged and made clean, good, and holy.

Some of us are smitten by our conscience. If you are convicted by your conscience, the blood of Jesus Christ, God's Son, can cleanse it.

We read in Romans 8:1, *"There is therefore now no condemnation to them which are in Christ Jesus."*

If you are a believer in Christ Jesus, say, "Lord, I am sorry. Forgive me." If you have not been faithful to God, let your conscience start all over again.

We have a saying, "Let your conscience be your guide." Do not believe it! The Bible is our guide. Your conscience is your relationship with God concerning good and evil. God has placed within you this mysterious thing called conscience. It understands good and evil. It will guide you to do the things that are good and will separate you from things that are evil. Your conscience is the scale of God's eternal justice.

36
The Birth of the Human Spirit

◆◆◆

*W*hat is the birth of the human spirit? The Lord Jesus Christ gave us the finest definition of it in John 3:3, *"Jesus answered and said unto him, Verily, verily, I say unto thee, Except a man be born again, he cannot see the kingdom of God."* That is one of the strongest statements in the Bible. Until this new birth comes, you cannot experience the kingdom of God. You are on the outside of God. You come to the inward parts of God only when you have experienced what Jesus called a "born-again" experience.

What Does "Born-Again" Mean?

John 3:4 says, *"Nicodemus saith unto him, How can a man be born when he is old? can he enter the second time into his mother's womb, and be born?"* We understand that at that time Nicodemus could have been ninety years old. His mother was probably dead. He was wondering how he was going to be born again. How could he enter into his mother's womb and be born a second time? This was a wise man. This was one of the members of the Supreme Court talking to Jesus.

"Jesus answered, Verily, verily, I say unto thee, Except a man be born of water and of the Spirit, he cannot enter into the kingdom of God" (v. 5). What did Jesus mean here?

He meant that when you are born of the water, it is a public testimony that you have come to God. It testifies that you have died to the things of the world, the flesh. It announces that you have come alive unto God. When you are born with a public witness, you are known by the blood of the Lamb and the word of your testimony. Water baptism is a word of testimony that we have truly been born again. So you have to be born of the water and of the Spirit. Unless you have done that, you cannot enter into the kingdom of God.

> *That which is born of the flesh is flesh; and that which is born of the Spirit is spirit.* (John 3:6)

> *Marvel not that I said unto thee, ye must be born again.* (John 3:7)

A New Heart

When a child is born into this world, the spirit element in him is dead because of his Adamic nature. We read in Ezekiel 36:26–27,

> *A new heart also will I give you, and a new spirit will I put within you: and I will take away the stony heart out of your flesh, and I will give you an heart of flesh. And I will put my spirit within you, and cause you to walk in my statutes, and ye shall keep my judgments, and do them.*

This is not the carnal man, neither is it the natural man. This is not the way a child grows up, because a child by nature is a sinner and a transgressor. A child will not normally tell the truth when it is convenient for him to lie. He will take what does not belong to him. When that new heart and new spirit come within him, he will walk in God's statutes and keep His commandments. These are two evidences that he has been born of the Spirit and a new person has emerged. How else can a man fulfill God's plan for his life? There is no other way. You can do anything else that you wish, yet you cannot perform what God wants you to perform without the new birth. The birth of the Spirit in our lives is the greatest and most important event that can take place in the life of a human.

The Spirit of Life

We read in Romans 8:10, *"And if Christ be in you, the body is dead because of sin; but the Spirit is life because of righteousness."* When you come to the Lord Jesus Christ and are born again, the old ways and desires are dead, gone, and finished. Instead, there is a spirit of life that brings about righteousness and causes you to walk, talk, and think right. The coming of God's Spirit into our spirit does something amazing for us.

Paul said further in Romans 8:11,

> But if the Spirit of him that raised up Jesus from the dead dwell in you, he that raised up Christ from the dead shall also quicken your mortal bodies by his Spirit that dwelleth in you.

The word *"quicken"* is an old English word that means that something is not dead; rather, it is alive, it moves, and it shakes.

An example of this is shown in the life of Noah. When Noah had gone through the Flood and had been in that awful ark for about a year, he wanted to come out of the ark. He let a dove out through the upper window to see if she could find a lodging place.

> *Also he sent forth a dove from him, to see if the waters*
> *were abated from off the face of the ground; but the*
> *dove found no rest for the sole of her foot, and she*
> *returned unto him into the ark, for the waters were on*
> *the face of the whole earth: then he put forth his hand,*
> *and took her, and pulled her in unto him into the ark.*
> *And he stayed yet other seven days; and again he sent*
> *forth the dove out of the ark; and the dove came in to*
> *him in the evening; and, lo, in her mouth was an olive*
> *leaf plucked off: so Noah knew that the waters were*
> *abated from off the earth. And he stayed yet other*
> *seven days.*   (Genesis 8:8–12)

Seven is God's spiritual number. Then Noah sent forth the dove that did not return. The dove did not return to the ark because there was a new creation on the face of that earth.

A New Creation in God

God also prepares a place in the Christian for Himself. It is a new creation. God wants us to move into that new creation with Him. He wants us to live with Him and do the things that belong to the Spirit of God.

If a person is a soulish Christian, then he is essentially what we call a worldly person. Worldly people are sinners and function only in body and soul. Soulish Christians have body, soul, and spirit; however, the human spirit is dormant so that the Christian is motivated by his soulical parts. God does not want that. God wants every Christian to be motivated by his spirit. He wants the spirit to be the king of your life. He wants you to obey the movements and operation of the spirit within you.

If you are a genuine Christian and active in God through your spirit, you do not live after the soul.

Instead, you live after the human spirit that God placed within you. Then your spirit is fused with God's Spirit and you have a hotline right into the throne room of God.

God's Spirit and Man's Spirit

In Romans 8, we see how man's spirit becomes one with God's Spirit. In the first seven chapters of Romans the spirit is seldom mentioned, but in chapter 8 it comes alive. You can hardly tell the difference between God's Spirit and man's spirit.

Instead of the Adamic soul controlling the spirit, the human spirit now controls the soul and the body.

Romans 8:11 says, *"But if the Spirit of him that raised up Jesus from the dead dwell in you, he that raised up Christ from the dead shall also quicken your mortal bodies by his Spirit that dwelleth in you."* God through His Spirit dwelling within us wants to command the body and the soul. The big question with so many Christians today is, "How do we function in the spirit and not in the soul? How do you get from moving in the soul to moving in the spirit?" Maybe a testimony would assist us. All of us have heard of the unusual Christian named Watchman Nee who said, "We must know that he who can work for God is one whose inward man can be released."

Releasing the Inward Man

The basic difficulty of a servant of God lies in the failure of the inward man to break through the outward man. God's Spirit that He has placed within you must break through the soulical parts (your mind, emotions, and will), and the physical senses (sight, hearing, taste, smell, and touch). If we have never learned how to release our inward man by breaking through the outward man, we are not able to serve the living God as we should. Nothing can so hinder us as the outward man dominating the inward man. When you become born again, your soulical part will not be king anymore. He lost his kingship and his preeminence. The inward man becomes the king, the dominant factor in your life. When you pray, you pray by your spirit. When you live, you live by your spirit. Your spirit becomes the real man within you. Christians are different from anyone else on the face of this earth because they are born-again creatures and their lives have been dominated by the Spirit of the living God.

Whether our works are fruitful or not depends upon whether our outward man has been broken by the Lord so that the inward man can pass through the brokenness. So many times we have to come to the Lord and say, "Lord, break us." What we mean is, "Cause the mind, emotions, and willpower to be subservient to You. Break down the old Adamic nature. Let the new life reign and rule in our hearts and lives."

Not being broken enough for the spirit-man to flow through into the soulical parts could be the basic problem of Christians today. The Lord wants to break our outward man in order that the inward man may have its expression visible to the world. When the inward man is released and the spirit begins to flow out, nonbelievers and Christians alike will be blessed. Everyone around us will be blessed because the inward man always brings blessing.

Moving to a Higher Plane

You are working on a higher plane when you live by your spirit. You are still using your soul when your spirit uses your mind, but your spirit is the dominant factor. The spirit knows more because it relates to both worlds. It relates to God and knows the mind of God; at the same time it knows what is best for the natural man. It is a double blessing when the spirit rules the life. Man was not supposed to eat of the Tree of the Knowledge of Good and Evil. God said it, but man disobeyed. This happened while Adam and Eve lived in the Garden of Eden. The soul then became overdeveloped. The Tree of Life would have been for the development of the spirit, but Adam and Eve never got that tree. All they had was the Tree of Knowledge of Good and Evil, which is related to the development of the soul. In the eternal life we are going to have the development of the spirit; we will be eating of the Tree of Life, and not just the Tree of the Knowledge of Good and Evil.

What Is Man's Basic Problem?

The overdevelopment of the soul or the inordinate affection of the soul has long been considered by great Christians as man's basic problem. If we are going to take the mind, emotions, and will and let them be kings in our life, then we are going to waver. If we do not work on a higher level, we will not be what God wants us to be. The soul can do many things. It can even put a man on the moon. However, it is utterly helpless in the things of the spirit. The soul cannot perform the works of the spirit. Your mind, emotions, and will absolutely cannot reach up to magnify and praise God like He wants to praised. He wants the spirit of man to do that.

We have an example in the Old Testament. When the children of Israel wished to offer themselves in full sacrifice to Jehovah, they did so by bringing a little pigeon, dove, or lamb as a sacrifice. This little animal or bird was to act as their personal sacrifice. The first thing the high priest did was to take a sharp knife and cut the offering into small pieces before the Lord. In the New Testament period, we do not bring doves, pigeons, and lambs to church. The real offering is within us. We must bring ourselves in full surrender. Even today, the procedure is the same.

A Sword to Divide

Jesus Christ, our high priest, takes a knife sharper than any Old Testament high priest ever had. He uses it to divide the spirit and the soul. The Word of God is living, powerful, and sharper than any two-edged sword; it pierces to divide asunder the soul and spirit. The Bible is the sharp sword that can discern and say, "Wait a minute; this is spirit, and this is soul. This is living by God, and this is living by Adam." Only the Word of God can teach us and show us exactly which is which.

Man is made in the image and likeness of God; he is tripartite: will, mind, and emotions. Try as you might, you will not find a fourth compartment of the soul. In the spirit we are also divided into three compartments: intuition (knowing without thinking it out as the intellect has to do in the soulical parts), communion (fellowship with the Father; His Son, the Lord Jesus Christ; and the Holy Spirit, which you cannot have without the born-again experience and your spirit coming alive), and conscience (inner witness to the Word of God). The body and the soul are subject to death because of sin, but the spirit is the substance of God.

The Father of Spirits

Hebrews 12:9 says, *"We have had fathers of our flesh which corrected us, and we gave them reverence: shall we not much rather be in subjection unto the Father of spirits, and live?"* God is the Father of spirits. The spirit in the unregenerate human is dead, or alienated from God. It is inactive, but that does not mean that it is extinct. The spirit, once renewed, is alive. It is clothed with a soul and a body, which become the media of expression for the spirit. The natural man is manifested and sustained in this life by his body. A sick body can destroy the manifestation of the mind. It can destroy the emotions. It can destroy the will. The human spirit enters reality only through the soul and body; likewise, the spirit exits the body by natural death or sin. The impartation of eternal life is through the soul and body; likewise, the spirit exits the body by natural death or sin. The impartation of eternal life is through the engrafted seed of the Lord Jesus Christ. James 1:21 says it this way, *"Wherefore lay apart all filthiness and superfluity of naughtiness, and receive with meekness the engrafted word, which is able to save your souls."*

First Peter 1:23 says, *"Being born again, not of corruptible seed, but of incorruptible, by the word of God, which liveth and abideth for ever."*

God Needs You—Spirit, Soul, and Body

There are three main words that describe the nature of man: his spirit, soul, and body. God needs all three of them. Man, through his body, can contact the outward world; he is world-conscious. Man, through his soul, is able to know himself; he is what we call self-conscious. In his spirit area, man has the capacity to know God; he possesses the capacity to be God-conscious. The three elements of the human personality are all needed.

Man is like a corporation. When you go into the factory, you see the assembly room where the people are putting the products together. This is comparable to the human body. In the office, you see the secretaries and the assistants working. This is comparable to the human soul. When you go into the president's office, you find the source of all the life and vision of the company. This is comparable to the human spirit. In the fallen man the governing office has been taken from the spirit and transferred to the soul of man. When the man comes back to God, he discovers a new world, a new life, and a new power.

"The LORD is nigh unto them that are of a broken heart; and saveth such as be of a contrite spirit" (Psalm 34:18). The spirit should be ruling the center of our personality. Whenever God does not rule in man's spirit, the spiritual personality lies dormant. It is not productive and does not produce a glorious, happy, fruitful Christian.

37
Life in the Spirit

◆◆◆

*I*f the soul becomes the king and ruler, it will destroy what the spirit builds. The soul must be broken before the spirit can be released to flow through a person's soul and body.

The Holy Spirit communicates with the human spirit. Besides Jesus, Adam was the fullest expression of the human spirit ever on the face of this earth. When Adam rebelled and disobeyed God, his spirit died. It ceased its relationship with God the Father. His actions and thoughts were now controlled by a body and by soulical parts. Then Satan began to control his personality.

That which perished in Adam was resurrected in Christ! We call that the "new birth." There are four words for "life" in the Greek language. One is *Bios*, the lowest form of life. There is *Psuche*, the soulical area. *Zoe* is the spiritual life, the Christ-life, the God-life, eternal life. This "Zoe life" is what John spoke of in 1 John 5:11–12, *"And this is the record, that God hath given to us eternal life, and this life is in his Son. He that hath the Son hath life; and he that hath not the Son of God hath not life."* The fourth of these is the *Anastrophe*, a confused manner of behavior used only once in the Scriptures.

The "Zoe Life"

In Christ we receive the "Zoe," the spiritual life, the divine nature. What we call the spirit of man is "Zoe life." The spirit of man is his born-again experience.

John 3:16 says, *"For God so loved the world, that he gave his only begotten Son, that whosoever believeth in him should not perish, but have everlasting life."* This speaks of the fusing of man's spirit with God's Spirit. The word *"world"* is one of those beautiful words that can mean the cosmos, the geographical earth, or the people. It is the people God loved. God loved the people so much that He gave His only begotten Son so that whosoever believed in Him would not perish. God wanted people to have life, the fusing of man's spirit with God's spirit. Ephesians 2:1 says, *"And you hath he quickened, who were dead in trespasses and sins."* The anointing comes when God's Spirit possesses the human spirit, and that spirit becomes renewed.

Ephesians 4:23 says to *"be renewed in the spirit of your mind."* This renewing must come out of your spirit and flow into your soulical parts. When this happens, your mind is cleansed by the blood of Jesus.

Ezekiel called it a new spirit. *"Cast away from you all your transgressions, whereby ye have transgressed; and make you a new heart and a new spirit: for why will ye die?"* (Ezekiel 18:31). God wants us to have that new spirit. This is the "Zoe life," the spiritual life, God's life.

In the Bible when a man received this new spirit, he would never again deal with men in his Adamic nature. Paul said he knew no man by the flesh.

What Is in a Name?

I have heard people speak of other people by saying, "Do you mean old Fatso?" You cannot know that man by the size of his body. Inside him might be a mountain of strength and God's might. His spirit might be tremendously alive. You must not know people after the flesh. We should know a person by his "Zoe life," by his spirit, by God's Spirit dwelling within him. Do not call people by ugly slang names.

We have a striking example in Jacob. "Jacob" was his soulical name. The name *Jacob* means "a person who takes from another." He liked to grab things that were not his. The word *Israel* means "a prince with God."

During Jacob's soulical times people called him Jacob. When he had his amazing conversion experience, the Spirit of God moved over him and the angel of God blessed him. The angel said, "You are no longer Jacob; you are Israel." After that people could not know him by his body, because his body was crippled. The angel hit him, and he forever dragged one leg behind him. People could have gone around saying, "There goes old crip," but they would have missed him altogether. Inside he was ten feet tall.

I lived in China for a long time, and they had a most interesting practice. They had secret nicknames for the missionaries. They would say, "Over in that missionary's home, the servant girl calls the mistress 'Tiger' in Chinese." The woman did not know that she was being called "Tiger." The names were picked because of the missionaries' personalities. We do not want to know people after their soulical parts. We want to know people by their spiritual beings. We want to know if they are strong in faith and love.

Ishmael was a son of the flesh. Galatians 4:23 says that he was of the bondwoman after the flesh. This son of the flesh was a thorn in the side of Abraham as long as he lived. Second Corinthians 10:3 says, *"For though we walk in the flesh, we do not war after the flesh."* Though we are related to the flesh, it is not a god, a king, or a ruler; it is under subjection to the "Zoe life" that comes from God.

Very often when you come to God, He gives you another name. The Lord Jesus encountered Peter and said, "I'll change your name. You were Simon; you are now Peter; you are a rock." Jacob's name was changed from "Supplanter" to "Prince of God."

Nowhere in the Bible do you have a description of the physical parts of Jesus. Matthew probably wanted to write down, "He stood six feet two inches, and His eyes were flaming and dark brown. The curves around His mouth were strong." The Holy Spirit said, "Rub it out." God was determined that we should know Him only by His spirit and not His body. He did not come for us to worship His body; He came for us to worship His Spirit. We are not to be like Him in our bodies; we are to be like Him in our spirits.

The Victorious Christian Energized by God's Spirit

The human spirit must be related to the glorious kingdom of God upon this earth. I could not give a definition for the spirit until God gave me Romans 14:17, *"For the kingdom of God is…righteousness, and peace, and joy."* We have the righteousness, peace, and joy of the kingdom. Isaiah said in Isaiah 12:3, *"Therefore with joy shall ye draw water out of the wells of salvation."* First Peter 1:8 says, *"Whom having not seen, ye love; in whom, though now ye see him not, yet believing, ye rejoice with joy unspeakable and full of glory."* That is your spirit. The human personality becomes a dwelling place of the Most High God. Man has only his spirit to deal with in the great issues of life. God wants your spirit renewed within you and strengthened within you.

Your spirit must grow stronger and stronger every day.

When I knew Smith Wigglesworth, he was eighty-five years old. Although his body could not run a race, his spirit could rise up like a giant within him. How glorious it was that his spirit was not getting weak with his body. He talked with such faith, such strength, such power, and such vitality, even at eighty-five years of age.

Numbers 14:24 tells us the secret of another eighty-five-year-old man who took an entire mountain single-handedly. *"But my servant Caleb, because he had another spirit with him, and hath followed me fully, him will I bring into the land whereinto he went; and his seed shall possess it."*

Then the children of Judah came unto Joshua in Gilgal: and Caleb the son of Jephunneh the Kenezite said unto him, Thou knowest the thing that the Lord said unto Moses the man of God concerning me and thee in Kadeshbarnea. Forty years old was I when Moses the servant of the Lord sent me from Kadeshbarnea to espy out the land; and I brought him word again as it was in mine heart. Nevertheless my brethren that went up with me made the heart of the people melt: but I wholly followed the Lord my God. And Moses sware on that day, saying, Surely the land whereon thy feet have trodden shall be thine inheritance, and thy children's for ever, because thou hast wholly followed the Lord my God. And now, behold, the Lord hath kept me alive, as he said, these forty and five years, even since the Lord spake this word unto Moses, while the children of Israel wandered in the wilderness: and now, lo, I am this day fourscore and five years old. As yet I am as strong this day as I was in the day that Moses sent me: as my strength

*was then, even so is my strength now, for war, both
to go out, and to come in. Now therefore give me
this mountain, whereof the LORD spake in that day;
for thou heardest in that day how the Anakims were
there, and that the cities were great and fenced: if so be
the LORD will be with me, then I shall be able to drive
them out, as the LORD said. And Joshua blessed him,
and gave unto Caleb the son of Jephunneh Hebron for
an inheritance.* (Joshua 14:6–13)

Caleb was a victor because of the spirit within him.

38
How the Spirit-Man Operates

◆◆◆

*J*ob 32:8 says, *"But there is a spirit in man: and the inspiration of the Almighty giveth them understanding."* The Almighty is the One who gives you your comprehension, understanding, movement, and operation. The Almighty is interested in your spirit. He directs, helps, and blesses your spirit area.

Your Spirit Has Its Own Personality

We read in Zechariah 12:1, *"The burden of the word of the LORD for Israel, saith the LORD, which stretcheth forth the heavens, and layeth the foundation of the earth, and formeth the spirit of man within him."* Just as He formed Adam and made him to be a living person, God formed the spirit within you. Your spirit has a personality that no one else has. You are an individual. You are as different from every other spirit as each snowflake is different from every other snowflake, or as every fingerprint is different from every other fingerprint. God is inexhaustible in His expression. Your spirit is related to God in the way that you yield to Him, making you different from any other person who ever lived.

There are over four billion people living on the face of the earth right now. Every one of those persons is different. There are no identical humans. The spirit within you is an individual spirit, and no other spirit is like that spirit. Every tender touch of God makes you different from someone else.

God forms the spirit within us by our reactions to His moving in our lives. Proverbs 20:27 says, *"The spirit of man is the candle of the LORD, searching all the inward parts of the belly."* God says your spirit is the light of the Lord on this earth. Sinners do not have this light.

We must arrive at a place where impulses and our inner emotions follow the living Spirit of God and not the Adamic nature. Our spirits are the candles of God on the face of the earth. We are the light of heaven. It is not your soul, mind, emotions, or will, but the newborn thing within you that is the candle of God. When you are born again, you become God's candle to light up the earth. *"Ye are the light of the world. A city that is set on an hill cannot be hid"* (Matthew 5:14). The headquarters and throne room of this new personality are in the cavity of the belly. Someone must sit on the throne; either God sits upon the throne or the devil sits on it.

James 2:26 says, *"The body without the spirit is dead."* It is spiritually dead. "Death" has many definitions; it does not always mean extinction. The father said of his prodigal son, "This is my son who was dead." (See Luke 15:24.) He was not off the face of the earth; he was separated from the father. So death can mean separation. God is telling us that the body without the spirit is inactive. It is not functioning. God said the spirit of man has to keep moving and living so the rest of our personality can function in God.

Power with God Is in the Anointing

I once knew an evangelist who had little or no education. He spoke King's English backward, sideways,

and a few other ways, but when he ministered under
the anointing of God, cancers would disappear before
our eyes. When I had a lump underneath my eye that
would not go away, he prayed for it. In a second it was
gone and never came back. I did not care what kind of
English he spoke; that had nothing to do with the lump
I could not get rid of. It was his spirit-relation that mat-
tered. If a man looks a little strange, peculiar, or backward, test the spirit. We should not judge any man
by his height, wealth, ingenuity, or the functioning of
a keen mind. We must know him by one thing, the
breath of the Holy Spirit that flows through him. If you
get to know people like that, you will have a bushel of
friends, and people will love you.

What Is Chemistry of the Spirit?

First of all, it is revelation. We use our spirits to
receive divine, eternal truth from God. For example, in
Matthew 16:17, after the disciple had said in verse 16,
"Thou art the Christ, the Son of the living God," the Lord
Jesus Christ turned to Peter and remarked, *"Simon...
flesh and blood hath not revealed it unto thee, but my Father
which is in heaven."*

Your spirit-man is the area in which you receive
spiritual revelation. You cannot receive spiritual revelation through your soulical parts. Many times we try
so very hard. We become so proud of our minds. Some
people actually worship their minds. Your natural man
will always seek to live naturally, but your spiritual
man wants to live by revelation. There are people who
are born again but cannot discern when the Spirit of
God is moving in a meeting and when it is another
spirit. In this revelation aspect, we must first know the
moving of the Spirit of God.

We must know when we are moving by God's Spirit, and when we are working with the soulical parts of our Adamic human nature. Many people have a lot more faith than they think. You meet people who are just boiling with faith inside, and the devil makes them think they have none. The devil says, "You do not have any faith," yet he knows they do. The devil never tells the truth. He is a liar and the father of lies. Through the spirit we realize our potential. We learn to believe "I am who God says I am. I can do what God says I can do." You function in your spirit-man through revelation. God says it, you believe it, and it works that way! In the chemistry of your spirit, revelation is important in realizing who you really are, and what your potential is. You cannot realize it through your brain. You might be able to do a thousand times more than your mind ever tells you that you can do.

39
The Abundant Life

—◆◆—

*H*ave you ever picked up the telephone, called a friend, and he answered with, "I was just going to call you"? That is intuition. You are flowing together. How many times have you been sitting by somebody and suddenly you said something and he said, "I was thinking the same thing"? That is the flowing together of the human spirit.

"For what man knoweth the things of a man, save the spirit of man which is in him?" (1 Corinthians 2:11). No one understands a human being until he knows the human spirit. Psychologists, as long as they believe that man is dualistic, made of two parts, will never truly understand the human person. If we do not get into the spirit movement, we will never understand truth like we should.

Knowledge through Revelation

Part of our spirit-man knows without learning. This knowledge without reason comes by revelation. You receive and perceive it, but it did not come through your mental faculties. It came through your spirit-man. You know it is true, and you are sure it is true, but it did not come through your reasoning power.

When I was in Alaska, I knew a man in his seventies who was what we call a "white Russian." He ran away from Russia because of the Communists. He had a shoe repair shop, and I would visit with him for long periods of time. One day he looked at me and said, "I want you to tell me something. I was sitting here in this shop praying, thanking God that I was a free man, and suddenly in my spirit I saw a funeral. It was a Russian funeral, but I was in Alaska. I looked into the casket, and there was my brother. They closed the casket, and the funeral guests walked away. I wrote it all down, and I wrote to Russia and told what I had seen. My brother's wife wrote back, 'Yes, you saw it, and from your letter you saw it the hour it took place.'" It is remarkable how our spirits within can move and do such things.

The devil has a counterfeit for everything God does. Just because there are a few ten-dollar bills floating around that are counterfeit, I am not ready to burn real ones. Just because there is a counterfeit, I am not going to downgrade the good. Here was a godly man who had run away from communist Russia because he loved God. The Lord was so kind to him that he awakened something within him in the same hour his brother was buried. He was at the ceremony by his spirit. There is a place in God where we can have a spiritual faculty. We know that we know. We are sure that we are sure. The power of God is what makes it manifest.

Can Others Perceive God's Spirit in You?

What are some of the divine expressions of the spirit of man within us? We send forth God's spirit to others by our spirit. Sometimes it is received and sometimes it is not. Once I was riding on a large airplane.

Normally when I fly, I work on my studies. I was just sitting there going through my studies when I glanced across the aisle, and there was a woman sticking her tongue out at me. I laughed, and she stuck her tongue out again. My spirit was moving around that plane and making her mad. I did not say a word. It was just my spirit. She was so full of evil she could not tolerate it. She could not put me off, we were thirty-seven thousand feet high, but she could stick her tongue out at me. You can be in the company of some people, and they get convicted of their sin by your very presence! On the other hand, you can heal people. You come into their presence and they say, "I just feel so good with you here."

Galatians 5:22–23 says, *"But the fruit of the Spirit is love, joy, peace, longsuffering, gentleness, goodness, faith, meekness, temperance: against such there is no law."* The fruit of the Spirit is the expression of the spirit of man. These are the fruit of your human spirit within you, not the fruit of your soulical man. These are the expressions and manifestations of the spirit that was born within you.

The gifts of the Spirit also reside in the spirit of man. When God gives you one of the gifts of the Spirit, it becomes resident in your spiritual part. It does not reside in your soulical part—your mind, emotions, or will—nor in the physical part. It lives in the spiritual part of you, and flows from your spirit. It does not flow from your natural person.

The Human Spirit Seeks Fellowship

What are some of the vital activities of your human spirit? A very beautiful one is fellowship. The human spirit, when it comes alive, seeks and finds relationships with like human spirits so they might flow together in the Holy Spirit. This fellowship occurs in prayer, song, and praise. In the total human being, man has physical contacts with the earth. Man can have fellowship through soulical contacts with his mind, emotions, and will. Man can also have contact with his spirit. He can flow with another in good things like the Word of God, song, the reading of the Word, prayer, praise, and so on. This is a great matter of fellowship.

First John 1:7 says, *"If we walk in the light, as he is in the light, we have fellowship one with another."* One of the activities of the human spirit is fellowship. We have fellowship with each other. Did you know the bonds of Christian fellowship are often much stronger than the natural bonds of blood? There are many people who will walk away from relatives in order to go to church and be with God's people. They say, "That is where I have my fellowship. We are all brothers and sisters in God. We are the same family and have fellowship one with another."

"But he that is joined unto the Lord is one spirit" (1 Corinthians 6:17). Once, in France, I was lost, and I could not speak French. I had to preach that night, and I did not know how to find the house where I was supposed to stay. Too many houses looked alike, and I could not knock on a thousand doors. I thought, "Well, all I can do is wander the streets until the police find me. I hope I can find somebody that speaks English." I stood on the street corner and began to pray, "Now Lord, I don't know who I'll ever find in this city that speaks English. I don't know how I'm going to find my way to church to preach tonight. Lord, You need to help." At that moment a man on a bicycle came by. He came up very close and said, "Hallelujah!" I said, "Oh, come here! Come here!" I knew "Hallelujah." I said, "I'm going with you." I did not know he was going to the church where I was to minister!

Try the Spirits

First John 4:1 says, *"Beloved, believe not every spirit, but try the spirits whether they are of God."* We live in the days when we need to try spirits and know what they are saying. We need to know if they are of God or not. Your spirit-man is the area of your personality that will reveal this.

"Speaking to yourselves in psalms and hymns and spiritual songs, singing and making melody in your heart to the Lord" (Ephesians 5:19). The activities of the human spirit are very special and very beautiful.

First Timothy 3:9 says, *"Holding the mystery of the faith in a pure conscience."* When God takes root in our conscience, He produces tremendous blessings of the Holy Spirit.

Paul says in 1 Corinthians 14:15, *"What is it then? I will pray with the spirit, and I will pray with the understanding also: I will sing with the spirit, and I will sing with the understanding also."* We have a right and are commanded to function with our brains and in our spirits.

Your Spirit Should Rule Your Soul and Body

When your spirit is born within you, it begins to grow up and become a mature Christian within you; it begins to rule and govern. It identifies the movements in your soul and body as to whether they are of God or not. It identifies whether your actions are spirit-fulfilling or soul-fulfilling. The spirit begins to utilize the soul and body for spiritual expression and manifestation.

You can gain strength, power, and victory in the workings of your spirit in the areas of unbelief. Many people struggle trying to believe something. When you are born again, you do not have to struggle at all; you just believe. I have no problems at all with believing. If you get a spirit of unbelief in you, you will not believe in your brothers and sisters. You will not believe what you hear—eventually you will not even believe the Bible.

In the spirit realm, we enter an area where we believe God. We enter an area where fear and confusion are gone. It is the work of the spirit within us to remove fears, phobias, unbelief, and demons. We call it reigning in heavenly places by the spirit.

Your spirit can keep growing. Your spirit is not full-grown the day you are born again. It has just begun to grow, and this is a continuing process. When your spirit and soul are right, they demand that the body become consecrated. That is when your total man functions in harmony with the Most High God.

Your Soul Activities Reveal the Born-Again Spirit in You

Your spirit can keep learning and growing your total life. Of course, your soulical parts can, too. Your mind will never cease to grow if you will let it learn new things every day of its life.

How do we know when we are receiving information from our spirit-man or our soulical man? How do you discern the spirit? Maybe this is the biggest of problems. We know whether we are dealing in the spirit or soulical parts of man by the source from which the information came. The spoken word reveals what is inside a person. The spoken word reveals whether or not he is walking in the spirit.

What you desire to read reveals your spirit. If you enjoy reading novels, shady materials, stories about broken homes, and pornographic literature, you are revealing the spirit inside you. Your reading material is a discerner of your spirit.

Your choice of companions reveals your spirit. When I got saved there was not a single one of my old companions who wanted to be anywhere near me. If you choose sinful companions, it is a sign you are not walking in the spirit.

Your worship reveals what you are on the inside. Some people only want dead, solemn worship. They think that worship has no relationship to joy, peace, happiness, or the flow of God. Church has to be dead or they cannot stand it. That is because they are dead. It is that simple.

Another indicator of your spirit is your meekness. Your inner person is revealed by whether there is a meek attitude or a stubborn one present in your personality. If you are stubborn, you are not walking in your spiritual man. Meekness and stubbornness in the same person reveals a split between the soul and the spirit.

40
The Spiritual Man in Final Battle

———◆●◆———

The great apostle said in Ephesians 6:10–12,

> *Finally, my brethren, be strong in the Lord, and in the power of his might. Put on the whole armour of God, that ye may be able to stand against the wiles of the devil. For we wrestle not against flesh and blood, but against principalities, against powers, against the rulers of the darkness of this world, against spiritual wickedness in high places.*

We do not wrestle with human persons; rather, we struggle against principalities, areas over which there is an evil prince. We struggle against powers that are not human. They are above humanity. We struggle against the rulers of the darkness of this world. We struggle against spiritual wickedness in exalted places, such as politics, religion, and economics.

Revelation 12:12 says,

> *Therefore rejoice, ye heavens, and ye that dwell in them. Woe to the inhabiters of the earth and of the sea! for the devil is come down unto you, having great wrath, because he knoweth that he hath but a short time.*

There is a final battle in the making. This decisive battle, the final battle, is the most important one. Whoever wins that last battle will have won it all!

The Time Is Now

We are living in the last moments of the Dispensation of Grace. I think we can feel the same as Babylon must have felt the last night of its history. I believe that people in Babylon were whispering to one another and saying, "There is an eerie feeling in the air." Doomsday was casting its shadows, and there were intelligent people who said, "We are getting to the end. Our king is feasting and drinking, but we are at the end of Babylon."

I believe that the citizens of Rome must have felt their doomsday when the fiery tongues of hell raced through the imperial city and Rome died. The people must have sensed the impending disaster upon the empire of Rome in its last dying, fiery moments.

Possibly the people in Jerusalem had the same feeling when their capital city was surrounded by the marching legions of imperial Rome. A commandment from the Emperor Titus said, "Burn it to the ground. Destroy it. Do not leave one stone upon another." The citizens of Jerusalem must have felt it!

Today you and I, as Christians, must be sensitive to the return of the Lord Jesus. I believe that we can feel the impending tribulation period as it approaches the world in which we live.

Be Ready

As Christians, you and I must prepare ourselves for the final attack of the enemy upon humanity. According to the Word, the devil is going to fight like a dying animal. He will do everything that he possibly can in his last great attack. Man will be at the very center of this final great battle. The battle will be in the area of the spirit of man. The spirit of man is the greatest part of man. It is the part of man that has intuition to know, love, and serve God. It is the part of man that has a conscience that he uses to know the Most High God, to serve Him, and to worship Him. The final great battle will be very strongly related to the spirit part of mankind.

Who Are the Faithful?

The Lord Jesus said in Luke 18:8, "Will I find faith on the earth when I come?" That means the spirit of man will be attacked. Something will try to destroy the spiritual faith of the human person. However, God's triumphant church will be able to fight the enemy and win in the spirit.

Millions of people will give themselves over to demon worship. The occult world is an attack on the spirit of man. It wants to steal his spirit away from God. Satanic worship and astrology are part of this last great attack on the human spirit.

The battle will be a spiritual battle to destroy the human spirit so that men will not be able to worship or serve God. Satan will come in such deceiving ways that many will not recognize him. His devices may seem so innocent, yet they will trap men's spirits so that they will not be able to worship God. This is why it is so important that we learn to live in our spirit-man and to keep constant and consistent fellowship with God. We will win in the final battle if, and only if, we live with the spirit as king and Jesus as Lord. By living in the spirit, we become that triumphant church against which the gates of hell cannot prevail. (See Matthew 16:18.)

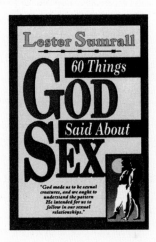

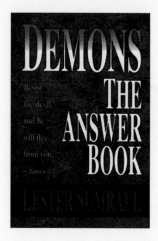

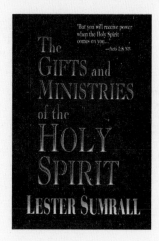